Al-Mutanabbi

SELECTION OF TITLES IN THE MAKERS OF THE MUSLIM WORLD SERIES

Series editor: Patricia Crone,
Institute for Advanced Study, Princeton

'Abd al-Malik, Chase F. Robinson
Abd al-Rahman III, Maribel Fierro
Abu Nuwas, Philip Kennedy
Ahmad ibn Hanbal, Christopher Melchert
Ahmad Riza Khan Barelwi, Usha Sanyal
Al-Ma'mun, Michael Cooperson
Al-Mutanabbi, Margaret Larkin
Amir Khusraw, Sunil Sharma
El Hajj Beshir Agha, Jane Hathaway
Fazlallah Astarabadi and the Hurufis, Shazad Bashir
Ibn 'Arabi, William C. Chittick
Ibn Fudi, Ahmad Dallal
Ikhwan al-Safa, Godefroid de Callatay
Shaykh Mufid, Tamima Bayhom-Daou

For current information and details of other books in the series, please visit www.oneworld-publications.com

Al-Mutanabbi

Voice of the 'Abbasid Poetic Ideal

MARGARET LARKIN

ONEWORLD
OXFORD

AL-MUTANABBI

Published by Oneworld Publications 2008
Copyright © Margaret Larkin 2008

All rights reserved
Copyright under Berne Convention
A CIP record for this title is available
from the British Library

ISBN 978–1–85168–406–9

Typeset by Jayvee, Trivandrum, India
Printed and bound in India for Imprint Digital

Oneworld Publications
185 Banbury Road
Oxford OX2 7AR
England
www.oneworld-publications.com

Learn more about Oneworld. Join our mailing list to
find out about our latest titles and special offers at:

www.oneworld-publications.com

FOR MY PARENTS, ORIGINAL AND SURROGATE

CONTENTS

Preface xi

1 OUT OF ARABIA 1
   Arabian origins 1
   Poetic forms – the ode 2
   Invective and elegy 3
   Poets on the fringe 4
   Islam's effect on poetry 5
   Centralization under the Umayyads 7
   Diversity under the 'Abbasids 8
   Conservatism in poetic taste 10
   Late 'Abbasid disintegration 11

2 GROWING PAINS 15
   Origins and early formation 15
   Al-Mutanabbi goes to Baghdad 17
   Early career in Syria 20
   Rebellion and its aftermath 23
   After the fall 25
   At Kharshani's court 26
   Death of the poet's grandmother 27
   The Ikhshidid connection 30
   Eye on the Hamdanid prize 31

3 GLORY DAYS IN ALEPPO 33
   The Hamdanids of Aleppo 33
   Al-Mutanabbi's first ode to Sayf al-Dawlah 35
   Occasional poems for the would-be patron 41

Death of Sayf al-Dawlah's mother 43
Elegy on Abu'l-Hayja' 46
The poet–patron relationship 50
Demands on the poet 52
Epic occasions 54
Trouble in paradise 57
Al-Mutanabbi bites back 60
All good things … 61

4 PARADISE LOST 63
From Aleppo to Egypt 63
Reluctant praise 66
Al-Mutanabbi demands his due 69
Saving face at Aleppo 72
Kafur's final refusal 73
Angry satire 75
Out of Egypt 76
Home again 78
Sayf al-Dawlah in the wings 80
The poet in Persia 84
The Gap of Bavvan 87
To the hunt 93
Final call 95

5 CONTEMPORARY CRITICS 97
After the fall 97
Linguistic correctness 98
Diction and lexical choice 99
Construction of the poem 101
Philosophizing in poetry 103
The limits of imagination 105
Borrowing versus plagiarism 107
Summing up 109

6 THE HIGHEST FORM OF PRAISE 113
Andalusian admirer 114
Kindred spirits 116
The classical as innovation 117
Neoclassical voice 121
Modern echoes 122

Conclusion 127
Suggestions for further reading 131
Index 135

PREFACE

Even al-Mutanabbi, renowned for his pride, ambition, and inflated aspirations, would have to acknowledge that time has given him his due. Few, if any, Arab poets' work has survived to be celebrated so long and by so many as the work of this tenth-century poet, generally acknowledged to be the last of the great poets in the classical Arabic tradition, and considered by some to be the greatest Arab poet. Born too late to participate in the grand literary efflorescence of imperial Baghdad during the eighth and ninth centuries, Abu'l-Tayyib al-Mutanabbi (d. 965 CE) assimilated the prevailing strains of the Arabic poetic corpus and distilled them in an *oeuvre* that would, for centuries, remain the model for Arab poets composing in the classical style. Among them were scores of poets in Islamic Spain from the tenth to the fourteenth centuries, who strove, Arabs and Jews alike, to emulate what they saw as the culmination of classical Arabic poetic culture. Those among them who excelled at their craft became known as the "Mutanabbi of the West." Modern poets writing in Arabic have continually invoked not only al-Mutanabbi's poetry but also his person as inspiration for their own verse and sense of identity as poets and have continued to refer to him, in the fashion of his eleventh-century successors, simply as "the poet." For them, his irrepressible personality and defiant individuality, which reshaped a poetry hemmed in by the constraints of convention would become the seed of artistic and psychological liberation that helped prepare the way for modernist Arabic poetry. More intriguing still, given the cavernous split between high Arabic and its elite literature on the one hand, and the vernacular dialects with their popular expression on the other, is the fact that al-Mutanabbi's verses have become woven into the fabric of everyday Arab life and are regularly quoted not only by aficionados, but also by more modestly educated people. An anecdote related by one of my former teachers, the late Professor Jeanette Wakin, in a graduate seminar at Columbia University, helps to convey the kind of power al-Mutanabbi's poetry holds in Arab culture, even today.

Jeanette (RIP) was an American-born child of Lebanese immigrants to the U.S. Like most immigrants, Jeanette's parents were keen to see their children prosper in their new country, and so when they found their daughter spending all her time on Arabic and Islamic studies, they were a little concerned about her future prospects, and her father did his best to re-direct his daughter's interests toward a more obviously promising career. He repeatedly asked her what she was going to do with all this Arabic, where it was going to get her, what kind of a job it would equip her for, and, try though she might, she was unable to convince him of the worth of her interests until one day she decided to memorize a few verses of al-Mutanabbi's poetry. The next time her father questioned her choice of studies, Jeanette did not try to reason with him or explain her choice, she simply recited the poetry for him, and watched as her father's eyes welled up with tears. The pragmatic immigrant, who had never been at a loss for arguments against the study of Arabic, fell silent and never again questioned his daughter's career path or her dedication to Arabic studies.

That is the emotional power that al-Mutanabbi's poetry has always had over speakers of Arabic. Both for privileged members of the educational and cultural elite, and for ordinary citizens with a more modest mastery of the Arab cultural tradition, the many gnomic verses sprinkled throughout the poet's *oeuvre* punctuate the events of their daily lives and seem eloquently to sum up the essence of life's struggles and emotions. Considered by many to represent the quintessence of Arab culture, al-Mutanabbi and his poetry have been the focus of numerous popular modern plays, and the poet even became the subject of an Iraqi television series in 1984. In 2001, the Baalbek International Festival in Lebanon (a world-renowned music festival, featuring Arab as well as western music and dance), which attracted over 40,000 people that year, opened with a musical – *Abu*

Tayeb al-Mutanabbi – by Mansour Rahbani, one of Lebanon's best-known musical artists, which featured some hundred dancers and performers.

Al-Mutanabbi and his poetry have been extensively studied, especially by Arab scholars. Kurkis and Mikha'il 'Awwad's extensive bibliography of editions, translations, and studies of al-Mutanabbi's poetry, *Guide to the Study of al-Mutanabbi*, covers over four hundred printed pages. Works such as Taha Husayn's *With al-Mutanabbi* and Mahmud Shakir's *Al-Mutanabbi* (by two of the leading literary scholars in the Arab world) are works of seminal importance for understanding not only al-Mutanabbi's poetry, but also the rich operations of intertextuality in the Arabic literary tradition. Among studies in western languages, Régis Blachère's 1935 *Un Poète arabe du IVe siècle de l'Hégire (Xe siècle de J.-C): Abou t-Tayyib al-Motanabbi* stands out as a masterful combination of biography and literary history. More recent works, which are listed at the end of the book in "Suggestions for Further Reading," have built on Blachère's foundation to add more in-depth historical and textual analysis to the communal stock of al-Mutanabbi studies. This work is the offspring of this communal legacy, on which it gratefully relies. More commentaries exist on al-Mutanabbi's *Diwan* (*Collected Poetry*) than on probably any other poet in the Arabic poetic tradition. Citations in the present text are to the commentary by al-Wahidi (abbreviated as "W.") (d. 1075 CE), which presents the poetry in chronological order. The poems themselves, which in Arabic do not carry actual titles, are referred to, as they are in the Arabic, by the initial phrase of the first line. Since space limitations preclude the inclusion of entire odes in this work, poetry citations are usually limited to brief sections of much longer works that serve to illustrate the stylistic features under discussion. A number of modern scholars, including A.J. Arberry, Régis Blachère, Andras Hamori, Geert Jan van Gelder, James Montgomery, Suzanne Stetkevych, Julia [Ashtiany] Bray, and others, have translated poems by al-Mutanabbi, most in the context of studies of his work. I have made use of these in producing my own translations, sometimes adopting them almost verbatim. These sources are all listed in the

"Suggestions for Further Reading" at the end of the book, and readers seeking lengthier poems in their entirety are urged to consult them.

In this book, I will analyze the main features of al-Mutanabbi's poetic style in the context of the diverse stages of his life and career, in the hope of explaining to some extent the generations-long mystique the poet has enjoyed. Some orientalist scholars unable to fathom the appeal of al-Mutanabbi's verse have peevishly questioned the taste of generations of Arabic speakers. The starting point for this book, in contrast, is my own unabashed admiration of his poetry.

It would be impossible to appreciate al-Mutanabbi's poetry without an understanding of the rich tradition of poetry that he inherited and the state of Arab culture and letters that he was born into. This, therefore, will be provided in chapter one. After a presentation in chapter two of al-Mutanabbi's family and educational background, as well as the early formative stage of his life and political activities, we will focus in chapter three on the heyday of his career as the court poet of the Hamdanid prince, Sayf al-Dawlah. The poetry al-Mutanabbi composed after he fled the intrigue-laden Hamdanid court, for patrons he deemed less desirable than Sayf al-Dawlah, forms the focus of chapter four. Chapter five discusses the intense critical debates concerning the merits and faults of his style among contemporary Arab critics. Before a brief conclusion, chapter six discusses the legacy of al-Mutanabbi's poetry in the centuries immediately following his death and in modern times, and suggests some reasons why it became such powerful intertextual currency for so many poet successors.

Sincere thanks go to Patricia Crone for inviting me to undertake this volume. I am likewise grateful to the American Council of Learned Societies and the National Endowment for the Humanities for an ACLS/SSRC/NEH International and Area Studies Fellowship that provided support during part of the time I spent working on this book, and to the Center for Middle Eastern Studies at Berkeley for a Sultan Fellowship that also contributed to the process. Special thanks go, as always, to Hussein for his patience and encouragement. Most of all, I thank al-Mutanabbi, for it was the sure knowledge that if I went to law school I would never again make time to read his magnificent poetry that kept me from taking what, for me, would have been a less fulfilling, if more lucrative, path in life.

OUT OF ARABIA

ARABIAN ORIGINS

For classical Arabic poetry, everything goes back to the desert. The earliest examples of Arabic poetry date from the late fifth or early sixth century, a little over a hundred years before the advent of Islam, though their formalized and sophisticated nature bespeaks a long history of earlier development. Orally transmitted and publicly performed compositions, this pre-Islamic poetry served, as the well-known expression goes, as "the register of the Arabs." The poets and their audiences were members of a tribal elite: rich, probably semi-sedentary, and politically and militarily dominant. The poetry constituted not only the record of tribal feuds and alliances, but also the vehicle for constructing a favorable public image for the poet's tribe and for reinforcing shared social and moral values. The importance of the poet in pre-Islamic tribal life is vividly described by Ibn Rashiq (1000–1063 or 1071 CE):

> Whenever a poet emerged in an Arab tribe, the other tribes would come and congratulate them. They would prepare food and the women would get together to play the lute, as they do at weddings, and the men and boys would announce the good news to one another. For a poet meant protection of their honor and defense of their reputations, memorializing of their glorious deeds and singing of their praises.
>
> (al-'Umda, vol. 1, 65)

POETIC FORMS – THE ODE

While the monothematic "occasional" poem was more abundant in pre-Islamic Arabia, the most prestigious form of poetry was the polythematic *qasidah*, or ode, the structure of which has remained more or less constant up to the present day. These poems consisted of monorhymed verses, usually thirty to about one hundred, divided into two half-lines or hemistichs, and employed any one of some sixteen quantitative Arabic meters throughout the composition.

More striking even than the regularity of its structure was the predictable stock of subjects treated in the pre-Islamic ode. Most often an ode would start with the scene of the poet stopping, sometimes with his companions – conceived to refer either to people or to the poet's sword and mount – at the site of his beloved's abandoned campsite. Features of the physical environment, such as traces like tattoos in the sands, evoked the memory of the woman who had once camped there with her tribe and the experience of loss occasioned by the tribe's departure. The lost beloved was then usually described in great detail. These amatory preludes and following paeans to the beautiful women are the only love poetry that we have from the pre-Islamic period. The poet-lover moved from the mood of loss and nostalgia evoked by this elegiac preface to a detailed description of his camel or horse, sometimes accompanied by descriptions of desert animals such as the oryx and the wild ass, and a depiction of an arduous desert journey. The mount, described as possessing consummate stamina, loyalty, and beauty, was often presented as a kind of alter ego for the wounded poet-lover, who recaptured his sense of strength and manhood through an extended and detailed homage to his animal. This process of recuperation came to fruition in the final movement of the poem, a series of verses in which the poet boasted the merits of his tribe and his named ancestors. The tribe was described as possessing all the qualities deemed praiseworthy in pre-Islamic nomadic society. It would be lauded for its unfailing generosity, its prowess and bravery in battle, and its sense of communal responsibility that demanded it provide protection to weaker tribes and individuals such as orphans and widows who sought support and protection. Poems composed in honor of the Ghassanid and Lakhmid kings, who ruled the Byzantine and Sassanian buffer states, concluded with a panegyric to the patron, and it is this poetry that most closely resembles the court poetry that was to dominate during later periods.

Recited publicly among groups of different tribes at caravan gathering sites, these compositions served as both an important vehicle for reinforcing the shared values and customs that held Bedouin society together and a potent form of propaganda and publicity for the various tribes. Poetry – in its content and performance context – constituted a communal voice, and the poet was little more than a representative, albeit a heroic one, of his tribe. Competition among the poets was keen, and, in keeping with the communal nature of the art, poets frequently borrowed from the compositions of others. This emphasis on intertextuality has remained one of the hallmarks of Arabic poetry, and we will discuss later how this inclination manifested itself in connection with the poetry of al-Mutanabbi.

INVECTIVE AND ELEGY

In addition to the boasting about the merits of specific tribes and their renowned members that was a standard feature of the polythematic ode, these compositions often included insults to members of enemy or rival tribes. Such verses, which also occurred as (usually) short compositions separate from the ode, generally consisted of a collection of coarse insults about not only the subject, but also the female members of his family. The public recitation and repetition of these poems was a key part of their functioning, since their purpose was to spoil the reputation and besmirch the honor of their target.

Poems of lament for the dead were also prevalent during the pre-Islamic period. Derived from women's rhymed prose wailing for members of their family, these compositions were somewhat less rigidly conventional than the ode. Among their frequently occurring features was that of the poet addressing her eyes and encouraging them to find relief in tears. The focus of the poem was praise of the deceased for his adherence to tribally sanctioned values such as bravery, generosity, and forbearance, followed by pronouncements about fate and the inevitability of death. The heart of the pre-Islamic social and moral code was belief in fate and its vehicle, time – or "the days" or "the night" – as the unseen, unfathomable arbiter of life, death, and everything in between in the desert environment.

Very little of the complete corpus of pre-Islamic and early Islamic Arabic poetry has come down to us. Any narrative we can produce about this poetry therefore necessarily involves filling in the blanks as best we can on the basis of what we do know. There are certain questions we will probably never be able to answer: for example, was there a body of poetry of a more popular nature than the prestigious ode form – perhaps poems composed in *rajaz*, the simplest of the sixteen recognized Arabic meters, such as the songs of the camel drivers? We simply do not have enough information to answer such questions fully. Though it is difficult to determine with any certainty how much of the corpus of pre-Islamic poetry was composed by the more sedentary members of Arab society – or indeed by over-zealous forgers during later periods – the essential ethos of nomadic life, its precariousness and its changeability, is nonetheless reflected in the themes and motifs of the surviving poetry.

POETS ON THE FRINGE

Not every poet of the pre-Islamic period was tribally enfranchised, and a body of compositions by *sa'alik* or "outlaw" poets (poets who had in some way fallen out with their tribe either because of their disillusionment with it or its disapproval and subsequent rejection of them) has also survived. For these poets, the tribal value system and communal ideals provided the overarching social and moral paradigm that they either rebelled against or defended from what they deemed the lax attention of tribal leaders. Some poets, such as

Ta'abbata Sharran, who probably lived during the first half of the sixth century, manifested a primitive individuality that distinguished their compositions from the main corpus of tribal poetry. These poems presented the image of a "man's man" tough enough to go it alone and face the elements of nature, finding companionship in the wild animals of the desert rather than his tribal comrades. The figure of rugged manliness they portrayed found impassioned reprise in many of the compositions of al-Mutanabbi, who obviously saw a kindred spirit in the world-weary tough guy that Ta'abbata Sharran described:

> I do not say when a friendship has been cut off
> "Woe to me," out of longing and compassion
> No! my weeping – if I am brought to weeping –
> is for a man skilled in acquiring praise, who is always ahead,
> Bare of flesh on the shins, the sinews of his arms standing out,
> often venturing out on nights that are inky black and pouring with rain.
> Such is the sort of man I care for and want [at my side].
> He is the one to whom I turn for help when I seek help –
> shockheaded and hoarse.
>
> (Jones, 1992, vol.1, 213–215)

ISLAM'S EFFECT ON POETRY

In its emphasis on the uniqueness of the Qur'an and the nature of Muhammad's message, the Qur'anic text repeatedly denies any relationship to poetry. Even though the new religion did not encourage poetry, the advent of Islam in the early seventh century provided an inadvertent spur to the field. Despite the ambivalence toward poetry expressed in the Qur'an and *hadith* (the sayings of the Prophet Muhammad), poetry was viewed as a treasure trove of information about the Arabic of the sacred text, and the fields of philology and lexicography blossomed. The text of the Qur'an emphasized the Arabness of the event of revelation and the kindness God had shown in revealing the sacred text in "clear Arabic" language. The need for linguistic information inspired the diligent collection and recording of poetry that, prior to Islam, had been preserved exclusively in the memory of professional transmitters attached to individual poets and conveyed orally. Islamic religious identity was thus very much Arab – Arab because the Qur'an had been revealed to an Arabian prophet, and Arab because the sacred text was in the Arabic language.

The connection between the word of God and the Arabic language persists today in the Muslim belief that although translations are acceptable to facilitate understanding among diverse groups of Muslim believers, only the Arabic text is the actual word of God. The notion, derived from specific verses of the Qur'an, that the text of the Qur'an is itself stylistically inimitable added to the emphasis on the language and, in part, shaped Arab attitudes toward rhetorical excellence in general. Thus, in the centuries immediately following the advent of Islam, pre-Islamic poetry increased greatly in prestige and became seen as the unquestioned model of excellent poetry. In later centuries astute critics, such as Ibn Qutaybah (828–889 CE) in his *Kitab al-Shi'r wa'l-shu'ara'*, rebelled against this notion that the more ancient the poetry, the better it necessarily was, but the overall thrust of conviction weighed in the direction of looking to the past.

After the death of Muhammad, Islam did not immediately expand beyond the confines of the Arabian peninsula. Leadership of the community remained in the hands of the close associates and successors of the prophet, who were themselves products of the same Arabian culture. Tribal affiliations and loyalties remained the well-spring of society. The new religion created a new bond that brought diverse tribes together in a community whose ties superseded the old tribal system, but old alliances and ancient animosities did not evaporate overnight. Indeed, the stature and circulation of pre-Islamic poetry, which exalted the tribal system with its loyalties and entrenched values, contributed to their perpetuation.

CENTRALIZATION UNDER THE UMAYYADS

After the establishment of the Umayyad dynasty (661 CE) – the first Muslim empire after the death of the prophet – things started to change for the young community. Muhammad left no instructions regarding the leadership of the Muslims after his death, so his succession became a thorny and divisive issue. Though even their leadership was not accepted without question, the first four, so-called "rightly guided," caliphs had the distinction of a personal relationship with the prophet to justify their authority. The Umayyad dynasty, initiated by the governor of Syria, Mu'awiyah, ushered in a distancing from the Arabian environment in which the religion had arisen. This was manifested physically by the transfer of the capital from Madina to Damascus, while Madina remained the center of religious scholarly activity. Meanwhile, Mecca, the birthplace of the prophet and the site of Muslim pilgrimage, was awash in new-found wealth and luxury.

For the first time, under the Umayyads, Arab tribes had to submit to the authority of a central imperial government. Wars of expansion into the former lands of the Byzantine empire in Syria and Iraq yielded spoils, and the mechanism of their distribution, in the form of money, became a bone of contention between the various provinces and the central government in Damascus. Arab Muslims involved in the campaigns of expansion came in contact not only with other Muslims from diverse tribes in the garrison towns established in conquered territories, but also with indigenous communities with their own religious and cultural traditions. The Arab tribal tradition of offering protection to tribes or individuals who became "clients" of powerful tribes continued with non-Arab converts in the conquered territories. This enhanced familiarity facilitated cultural assimilation, and the complacency of an ethnically homogeneous society was gradually disappearing. At the same time, the young community of believers was still sorting out what it meant to be a Muslim and what kind of organization the community should have now that its founder and prophet was no longer among them. The factionalism that challenged the community was as often religious and political in nature as it was tribal.

Despite – or perhaps partly because of – this general opening up of Arabian tribal society and the many social, political, and economic transformations it was undergoing, Arab poets in the century following the death of Muhammad clung to essentially the same poetic conventions as had prevailed in pre-Islamic Arabia, especially where the polythematic ode was concerned. There were developments toward a more straightforward and simple language in the occasional, monothematic poem, and both the love poem and the wine-song blossomed at this time. The major change that took place in the ode was in its performance context. With the exception of panegyric poems in honor of the pre-Islamic kings of Hira (the Arab buffer state bordering western Mesopotamia), pre-Islamic odes were generally performance pieces in which praise was reserved for the poet's tribe or outstanding individual members of the tribe. Now for the first time praise poetry was composed and performed in honor of kingly rulers who paid for the good press that these compositions provided. As in the pre-Islamic period, poetry served as propaganda; the big difference was that the publicity now often served the purpose of bolstering the image of the central Muslim authority and legitimizing the caliph and his evolving Muslim world-view. Traditional tribal values were being re-cast in religious and political terms befitting the new Islamic communal realities, including their tensions and controversies.

DIVERSITY UNDER THE 'ABBASIDS

This trend became even more pronounced during the 'Abbasid era, the first two centuries of which (early eighth to the early tenth century) represent the heyday of Arabic letters, including poetry. This dynasty, which claimed legitimacy on the basis of descent from al-'Abbas ibn 'Abd al-Muttalib, the uncle of the prophet Muhammad, capitalized on a widespread frustration with the Umayyad rulers. Accusations of authoritarianism, nepotism, and lack of piety had undermined Umayyad rule and united Arabs and non-Arabs in the goal of ousting them. The challenge of shaping a unified Muslim polity from the diverse communities that were included in the now far-flung Muslim empire was beyond Umayyad moral and political abilities. By now, the majority of Muslims were non-Arab and urban, the desert and its tribal ethos little more than a distant memory. Under the 'Abbasids, the old Arab families that had spearheaded the Muslim military drive for expansion no longer received the preferential treatment they had enjoyed under the Umayyads, and the many Arabized Persians and others who had converted to Islam were more integrated in 'Abbasid life. The social and political structure of 'Abbasid government was centralized around the caliph and an extensive bureaucracy that was essentially run by Persians and Aramaeans. With the establishment of the capital at Baghdad in 762 CE, the Muslim community not only gained a grand imperial court but also a vibrant cultural center, in which virtually all fields of scholarship and art were sponsored. The golden days of 'Abbasid patronage reached their height under Harun al-Rashid (r. 786–809 CE), whose era boasted some of the most outstanding poets of the time, including Abu Nuwas (ca. 755–813 CE) and Abu 'l-'Atahiyah (748–826 CE).

In the multi-cultural environment of the 'Abbasid caliphate, where many of the outstanding poets were of Persian origin, the poet's stock-in-trade was his ability to produce compelling panegyric poems that served to legitimize and aggrandize the caliph and his officials or whoever was wealthy enough to engage the poet's services. Despite the powerful claim of genealogical ties to the prophet, the 'Abbasid caliphate, which had been brought to power by the Persians of Khurasan, needed to present itself to the Muslim public as a faithful adherent to ancient Arab tribal values. Some of the grander odes of this period, produced by poets such as Abu Tammam (ca. 805–845 CE), portray the 'Abbasid caliph as possessing traditional Arab heroic qualities, such as generosity and bravery, and also attributes associated with Sassanian and ancient Near Eastern models of kingship. In these mythologizing descriptions, the caliph was often depicted as having power over the natural world, so complete was his appointment from God. Where fate had been the explanation for everything in the pre-Islamic poetic universe, Islam now took over that role. In that sense, 'Abbasid panegyric poetry in honor of caliphs was not just publicity for the individual ruler, but also an expression and public reinforcement of a shared Islamic world view, and played a vital role in furthering social cohesion.

CONSERVATISM IN POETIC TASTE

Despite profound changes in the ethnic makeup of the Islamic empire during the eighth and ninth centuries, the fact that the major practitioners of the traditional Arab art of poetry were Persians, and most of them urbanites who had rarely, if ever, set foot in the desert, poets were expected to cling to the sacrosanct conventions of pre-Islamic Arabic poetry, only minimally adjusted to accommodate the new reality of their audience. The tripartite ode, still the dominant poetic form, usually opened with an amatory prelude with the customary stopping at the abandoned campsite of the lost beloved, usually followed by a journey section in which the poet's mount was painstakingly described. The catalogue of travails encountered during this journey over harsh terrain was meant, in the 'Abbasid ode, as an incentive to increased generosity on the part of the patron who had commissioned the work. The traditional praise section of the pre-Islamic ode was retained during the 'Abbasid era in the form of exaggerated praise of the patron, in which his tribal origins were elaborately vaunted. It mattered little whether the patron actually possessed the enumerated virtues, for praise poetry was a ritual performance that did not have to meet the test of truth. Many a member of the new middle class of merchants that had emerged during the 'Abbasid era found himself portrayed as a greater-than-life hero in poetry he was happy to reward generously. A number of outstanding poets, foremost among them Abu Nuwas, rebelled against this oppressive adherence to tradition and mocked the stultifying conventions derived from desert society.

The premise of the prevailing conservatism in poetry was the belief that the ancient poets had said just about everything there was to say, leaving the so-called "moderns" with nothing to do but find clever and appealing ways of expressing the same ideas. "Ideas," as the ninth century polymath, al-Jahiz, so succinctly put it, "are strewn in the road." This was not a new sentiment: pre-Islamic poets such as 'Antarah and Imru' l-Qays wondered in their poetry whether their predecessors had left anything for them to say. In the 'Abbasid era, the situation was much more acute. The inevitable result of this thinking was an era of manneristic poetry, in which poets composed works that focused primarily on novelty of expression rather than meaning. In poems that can best be likened to the works of the English metaphysical poets, 'Abbasid poets employed an abundance of rhetorical figures and emphasized abstract, and sometimes far-fetched, conceits. This self-consciously clever poetry did not escape the criticism of the critics; poets such as Muslim ibn al-Walid, Bashshar ibn Burd, and Abu Tammam were criticized for their extravagant use of punning, double entendre, and antithesis, among other figures. This was the age of Hellenist-inspired rationalism, and many of the important poets of the era were clearly influenced by the methods of the Muslim speculative theologians. Evidence of infatuation with logic and manipulation of philosophical concepts in their poetry was often sufficient to invite censure or even charges of heresy. One of the more far-reaching innovations of the practitioners of the so-called "new style" (badi') poetry was their tendency to manipulate figures such as antithesis as structural features organizing entire poems. Since, as the poet and critic Ibn al-Mu'tazz (861–908 CE) pointed out in his treatise on this poetry, the same rhetorical figures can be found in the Qur'an and in the poetry of the "ancients," they were not, in and of themselves, novel. Rather, it was the modern poets' excessive dependence on them that roused the ire of some of the 'Abbasid critics.

LATE 'ABBASID DISINTEGRATION

The Islamic world into which al-Mutanabbi was born in 915 differed greatly from the golden age of the 'Abbasid caliphate. Al-Mutanabbi appeared on the scene during the breakup of the 'Abbasid caliphate and the disintegration of Arab absolutism. Gradually undermined by foreign armies employed by the caliph, the 'Abbasids lost virtually all authority over the vast lands of the once-unified Islamic empire. With the decline of the strong agricultural base of the economy, which had traditionally thrived on the "black" soil of lower Iraq, the 'Abbasids were unable to retain control of their expansive territories and support their elaborate central administration. Persistent unrest – in the form of rebellions among the black slaves who worked the agricultural land, among the 'Alids, who felt that only 'Ali ibn Abi Talib (a descendant of Muhammad through his cousin and son-in-law) should lead the Muslim community, and the Qarmatians, pretenders to the caliphate who were wreaking havoc in Syria and Iraq – disrupted the peace and security of the empire and placed military demands on the caliphate that it could not meet. Little by little, the Muslim empire was shrinking, its territories either parceled out in fief-like chunks by the 'Abbasids as temporary solutions to large financial problems, or usurped by the armies of more powerful independent principalities. The caliph, reduced by the early tenth century to the status of little more than a figurehead, was increasingly unable to defend the empire against the Byzantines, who were constantly trying to regain territories lost to the Muslims.

The implications for Arabic letters were enormous. The breakup of the 'Abbasid caliphate lead to a proliferation of new local courts that served as important hubs of culture sponsoring diverse types of literature, with Arabic as the language of high culture and court administration. Although the death of Baghdad as a cultural center lagged behind its political and military demise, the dissolution of the 'Abbasid core of power in Baghdad represented the loss not only of an important cultural and intellectual melting-pot where scholars of any ilk could meet, study, and collaborate, but also the loss of a potent symbol of Arab cultural unity. The idea of the Arab hero uniting a vast and multi-cultural empire of believing Muslims was gone forever. For example, when the Buyid dynasty, which ruled the most influential confederation of principalities born out of the 'Abbasid ashes, exalted Arabic poetry, – which it did vigorously in many of its provincial courts – it was none the less a Persian dynasty, which paid little more than lip service to the 'Abbasid caliphate, celebrating the Arab cultural tradition. Though al-Mutanabbi was to find, in the Buyid prince 'Adud al-Dawlah, the kind of deferent indulgence and generosity that he required, along with sincere admiration of his poetry, he remained discontented with this essentially Persian environment that lacked a deep-seated sense of identification with Arab culture and values. In truth, al-Mutanabbi was temperamentally suited to an earlier age – to an age that was not just Islamic, but also essentially Arab.

The economic ramifications were also serious for poets. In an era when the dominant poetic mode was panegyric, and when poets made their living by eulogizing wealthy and influential patrons, the diminishment of the powerful cultural center of Baghdad was significant. Baghdad still had its poets, and continued to exert a measure of influence over the course of their careers, but the situation was a far cry from what it had been. Gone were the days when a talented self-starter could find his way to Baghdad and there, with the support of powerful patrons and influential scholars, find both fame and fortune; the aspiring poet now had to cast his hopeful net more widely to find the necessary support for his art.

For al-Mutanabbi, the psychological ramifications were tremendous. This tenth-century poet was deeply attached to the image of the Arab hero who represented the perfect combination of tribal values of bravery and generosity, battling in the name of Islam against its non-Muslim enemies. It was not that the age he lived in provided al-Mutanabbi with diminished opportunities for wealth and prestige, but that it lacked the heroic patron he so longed for. Sayf al-Dawlah (r. 945–967 CE), the leader of the northern Syria branch of the Hamdanid dynasty, would eventually represent for al-Mutanabbi the longed-for ideal Arab hero he had thought was no longer to be found. But until that association came into being, he had to make a living, and that required seeking out rich patrons whose reputations would be enhanced by being panegyrized by a talented poet. Al-Mutanabbi's early professional life was a series of frustrations, as he travelled around seeking a long-term and satisfying relationship with a patron. During his days as an itinerant panegyrist, he lauded numerous wealthy bourgeois, but failed to establish a sustained relationship with anyone he deemed a worthy sponsor. Even during his early days, al-Mutanabbi had a clear sense of his own greatness and imagined himself a great Arab hero of the type he would later glorify in his poetry. But before we take a look at the frustrations and adventures of al-Mutanabbi's early career, we need to paint a clearer picture of his background, his education, and the social and political environment that shaped him.

GROWING PAINS

ORIGINS AND EARLY FORMATION

The Iraqi city of Kufa had had a long history of religious and political dissent by the time Abu'l-Tayyib Ahmad ibn al-Husayn al-Ju'fi al-Mutanabbi was born there in 915 CE. Since its brief stint as caliphal capital under the fourth caliph, 'Ali, the city had been a stronghold of Shi'ite support. In the ninth century, it had been the site of one of the two main schools of philology, and a center of both Islamic and pre-Islamic tradition collection. In short, it was an intellectually dynamic environment, with a strong history of religious and intellectual independence, to which al-Mutanabbi would contribute dramatically.

Though the chain of al-Mutanabbi's genealogy breaks off fairly early, and doubts about the purity of his origins have been raised, the poet's family seems to have stemmed from a south Arabian tribe who were Shi'ite in leaning. This Yemenite origin was a source of pride to al-Mutanabbi and, pointing to the excellence and south Arabian origin of his renowned predecessors, Abu Tammam (d. 845 CE) and al-Buhturi (d. 897 CE), he even suggested that the Yemenites possessed an innate and unique talent for poetry. Little is known about the poet's mother, who seems to have died very early in his life, for he was raised by his grandmother.

Al-Mutanabbi's family was poor. The accusations that his father was a lowly water-carrier may have some validity, since he lived near a district in Kufa that was inhabited by weavers and water-carriers.

Given this supposed poverty, it is curious that the school al-Mutanabbi attended was a Shi'ite-leaning one known to be patronized by the best families in Kufa. This, along with the attention the family received from a well-known 'Alid patron, has led some to give credence to claims that the poet was connected to the 'Alid nobles of Kufa and therefore a member, if at some remove, of what would be considered a noble caste in Kufan culture.

Al-Mutanabbi was a *Wunderkind*. His obvious natural talents were matched by a studious personality, and he became famous for his prodigious memory. In a primarily oral scholarly culture, the ability to memorize texts – not just poetry, but also diverse scholarly treatises – was highly valued, and the medieval sources provide numerous anecdotes about people with impressive memories, including al-Mutanabbi. On one occasion, tradition has it, al-Mutanabbi was in a bookseller's shop when the owner of a treatise by the philologist al-Asma'i came in to arrange to sell the book. While he was negotiating with the bookseller, al-Mutanabbi started reading the work, and when he demonstrated that he had memorized the thirty-page treatise during the brief time the owner was speaking with the bookseller, the owner gave it to him as a gift in recognition of his impressive memory. Al-Mutanabbi's poetic talents manifested themselves from a very early age. In Arab culture, where poetry was prized more than any other art form, al-Mutanabbi was thus a precocious star. Some of his youthful compositions have been preserved, despite the purging his *diwan* (collected poetry) underwent at his own hand, though it is impossible to date them with any certainty.

When al-Mutanabbi was about ten years of age, his family left Kufa to stay for two years with the Banu Kalb tribe in the Samawah region of the Syrian desert. While the family may have been fleeing the turmoil left in the wake of the Qarmatian sacking of their native city in 924 CE, for al-Mutanabbi the two-year stay with the Bedouin constituted the important basic training sojourn that had become customary among poets of the period, who viewed the Bedouin as the preservers of the purest form of the Arabic language. On his return to Kufa, al-Mutanabbi became attached to Abu'l-Fadl, a Kufan, credited with introducing the young man to Hellenistic philosophy, perhaps specifically the Shi'ite gnostic teachings that were circulating in the area at that time. This verse from a poem in praise of this mentor, in which al-Mutanabbi likens Abu 'l-Fadl to God, is an early instance of the sacrilegious tone often found in the poet's verse.

> I behold you, though I think I must be dreaming
> [But] who could dream of God, that I might be dreaming [of him] now?
>
> (W., 20)

In early 929, at the age of fourteen, the promising young poet, perhaps accompanied by his father, set out for Baghdad and his first turn at finding fame and fortune in the 'Abbasid capital. He left behind the only mother he had ever known, his beloved grandmother, whom he was never to see again.

AL-MUTANABBI GOES TO BAGHDAD

Baghdad, at this point in history, was a shadow of its former grand self, and the talented newcomer found little substantive support for his poetry in the political disarray of the ailing capital. The patron of one surviving ode, Muhammad ibn 'Ubayd Allah, who was an 'Alid businessman and landowner from Kufa, is representative of the type of patron al-Mutanabbi was able to acquire during this early stay in Baghdad. The forty-two-line poem, eulogizing Ibn 'Ubayd Allah, allows us to assess the state of the young poet's art. The ode seems to be standard neo-classical fare, employing all the traditional motifs of the polythematic ode, but there are some telling details forecasting trends that would dominate in al-Mutanabbi's later compositions.

Though many of al-Mutanabbi's works, even early ones, omit the traditional amatory prelude, this poem commences in traditional fashion. As Andras Hamori (1992) has pointed out, al-Mutanabbi tended to retain this amatory opening for praise poems that were not occasioned by particular large battles or other events. But here already our poet is nipping at the edges of the conventions that he would more boldly challenge later in his career. In pre-Islamic poetry, one of the conventional motifs consists of reference to two companions whom the poet-lover addresses and invites to pause with him over the remains of the lost beloved's campsite. This does not occur in every pre-Islamic poem, but where it does, it is an integral vehicle of the pathos of the amatory prelude, with the customary crying over the effaced campsite. In this ode, al-Mutanabbi invokes this convention, but with a significant little twist: instead of apostrophizing two companions who would share his grief with him and urge him to recover from it when the time was right, the poet addresses the two camel-drivers leading away the beloved, in what would otherwise be the familiar scene of departure of her tribe. He calls on them to halt the departure that is, literally, in their hands and allow him a brief glance at the woman who will soon be gone from his life. The effect of this slight manipulation of the convention is to render the traditional scene ever so slightly more dynamic. The two men being called on to halt would actually have some power to re-direct the scene. Unlike the two companions of the tradition who are as powerless as the poet, the camel-drivers are able to alter events and potentially rewrite the script of this conventional scene. Al-Mutanabbi is breathing a bit of new life into the convention: for the brief moment when the camel drivers are addressed, the entire set progression of the conventional scene is called into question. The poet is simultaneously drawing the listener's attention to the rigid predictability of the conventional motif and to the potential for change suggested by his subtle manipulation of it.

A similar instance of tweaking the conventions occurs in the description of the poet's camel. In this poem, the novelty is that the mount is not a camel, but rather the poet's feet, his only means of transportation, and he likens the parts of his sandals to the various parts of the camel and its appurtenances. The flavor of this section, where the poet describes himself as running as fast as the wind, is reminiscent of the poetry of the *sa'alik* – or "outlaw" poets – who vaunted their ruggedness, speed, and ability to face the elements alone. This poem is both a thorough display of al-Mutanabbi's precocious virtuosity and his mastery of the pre-Islamic and

Islamic poetic corpus and an announcement of his great potential as innovator.

Several stock features of his style are already apparent. For example, his great economy of expression and his ability to convey several key ideas in one concise formulation is apparent in line 29:

> The people know with certainty that he who planted it
> through cunning, will reap its harvest in his [own] heart.
>
> (W., 13)

The poet is focusing on a mark left on his patron's face as a result of a wound suffered in battle. Al-Mutanabbi's goal is to portray this visible sign of partial defeat or weakness as a positive thing. Line 29 is the culmination of a four-line treatment of the patron's wound. In it, the poet condemns the enemy who managed to wound his patron, by declaring him a coward for having sneaked up on him instead of facing him – he planted the blow "through cunning" – while implicitly praising Muhammad ibn 'Ubayd Allah – for the enemy would not have been able to wound him except through cunning. Had he faced him bravely, the courageous patron would, of course, have won the day. The poet also asserts that Muhammad ibn 'Ubayd Allah, in true Arab warrior fashion, will avenge this perfidious assault. Al-Mutanabbi here assumes the traditional role of the Arab poet as publicist for his subject, with his description of the public reaction to his patron's wound serving the performative function of instructing the public as to what their view of his patron should be. This verse, though not terribly original, is laden with ideas stemming from the Arab tradition. In his very condensed formulation, al-Mutanabbi manages both to paint the picture of a complete Arab hero possessing all the traditionally admired traits, and to place himself within that same tradition as the monitor of and spokesperson for shared social values.

Al-Mutanabbi's favorite rhetorical figure, antithesis, is early displayed in this poem, for example, in line 34:

> Fire is kindled from the places where they (the swords) strike
> While the water of their necks (i.e., the enemies' blood) extinguishes it.
>
> (W., 14)

The line, built on the opposition of the two verbs, "to kindle" and "to extinguish," and the contrast between the two named elements, "fire" and "water," accomplishes several goals. The antithesis draws attention to the inherent irony in the situation – to the idea that it is in the nature of fierce battle to bring together opposites, to shock and be chaotically forceful. The use in this figure of elemental substances such as water and fire emphasizes the primal power of intense battle. Furthermore, by assigning the patron power over these opposing elements, the poet is describing him as arbiter over life and death, as if he possessed virtually cosmic power. This notion is elaborated in the next few lines of praise in the poem, as al-Mutanabbi concludes his hyperbolic praise of Muhammad 'Ubayd Allah in a fashion that elevates his merit to a higher plane. Ibn 'Ubayd Allah does not just possess physical might, but also spiritual authority, while his enemies are on the wrong side of the true path, and his excellence is such that all creation acknowledges it. This combining of material and spiritual authority, sanctioned by creation and the natural world, is an echo of what Abu Tammam, al-Mutanabbi's famous predecessor, did in some of his odes, in which he raised his caliph-patron to a cosmic level of authority and singularity. In the concluding verses of this ode al-Mutanabbi, already assuming the prerogative of the confident panegyrist, takes on the role of judge of what true generosity is and invokes the traditional power of the poet to make or break someone's reputation for liberality, while also encouraging his patron to be as generous as possible in rewarding him for the poem.

EARLY CAREER IN SYRIA

After his stay in Baghdad, al-Mutanabbi spent two years in Syria, where his experience was scarcely better than it had been in the capital. In Latakia, where he was attempting to establish a patronage relationship with the Tanukhis – an illustrious family of litterateurs, judges, secretaries, and transmitters of prophetic sayings – al-Mutanabbi composed a number of poems that convey not only his great ego, but also his profound pride in his south Arabian tribal origins. At the same time, the persistent difficulty in interpersonal relations that al-Mutanabbi would have throughout his life is clearly foreshadowed. His attempt to gain the sustained patronage of the Tanukhis failed in part because of the effort of detractors, who composed a satire of his would-be patron the governor of Latakia and ascribed it to al-Mutanabbi. Although al-Mutanabbi composed a poem in which he responded to these slanderers and disavowed their inferior poetry, the damage had been done.

The poetry of this early period is revealing in two ways: it conveys a clear picture of the immense promise of this young poet, and of his complex personality. Not only was al-Mutanabbi extremely proud and ambitious, he was also a racial elitist, disgusted to see Arabs subject to the authority of non-Arab rulers. As he declares in a panegyric to 'Ali ibn Ibrahim al-Tanukhi:

> People [are measured] by their kings
> And no Arabs whose kings are non-Arab will ever prosper.
>
> (W., 148)

In this piece ("Oh, continuously raining [cloud] …"), the conventional amatory prelude is replaced by the poet's complaint about the contemporary political situation and his own personal fate, followed by his trademark boasting:

> Though I blame my enviers
> still I do not deny that I am a punishment to them.
>
> (W., 149)

This is a tack he was to develop and elaborate throughout his career, gradually replacing the communal voice of pre-Islamic poetry with a clear individual voice and personal presence, even in panegyric poetry. Even in this fairly desperate period of his professional life, al-Mutanabbi often produced panegyrics that focused as much on himself as they did on his patrons. As we will later discuss, this was a revolutionary change, which did not escape the grateful attention of generations of admirers. It is easy to imagine how difficult it must have been for such a haughty young man to wander from one potential patron to the other in the hope of finding stable patronage. Some of the satire/invective poems al-Mutanabbi produced during this period seem to owe their origin to the rough reception he received from some potential sponsors. Far from easygoing, al-Mutanabbi was often at odds with the customs of sociability, and his dislike of drinking made him the butt of jokes by potential patrons and their associates. Given his pride, it is not surprising to find al-Mutanabbi justifying his abstention from alcohol by a heroic self-portrait, as in the following epigram composed, extemporaneously, to decline the invitation of a friend, Abu Dabis:

> More pleasant than choice old wine
> and sweeter than handing round cups
> Is handling broad swords and tall lances
> and me thrusting an army into another army
> To die in battle is my life, for as I see it
> [attaining] the soul's need [alone] is living
> But if I could be served wine by the hands of a
> companion and be pleased, he would have to be Abu Dabis.

(W., 86)

It is clear from this that al-Mutanabbi fancied himself a warrior. Interestingly, while he does describe himself as a great poet – "the master of rhymes" – it is primarily the image of himself as a hero on the battlefield that he nurtures. The great irony is that, according to some sources, at this point in his life he was barely able to mount a horse or assemble his weaponry. It would, I believe, be wrong to read, as some scholars have, the bluster of this exaggerated self-image as a psychopathology. Throughout his life, the greater the insult he had to endure, the haughtier al-Mutanabbi became, and there is no doubt that his pride was seriously wounded by his early difficulties in finding patronage. A child prodigy, he probably expected the world to throw open its arms to him, which is hardly what happened.

The craftsmanship of much of al-Mutanabbi's early poetry is so accomplished that it is difficult to remember that he was just a teenager, though there are a few pieces that are almost refreshingly adolescent. Warned by concerned friends that he should stick to praising great men and leave off the tirades, al-Mutanabbi, like a typical rebellious teenager, responded with increasingly bold expressions of defiance:

> So leave me my sword, my steed and my supple lance,
> as if we were one, to confront men [in battle] – then watch what I will do!
>
> (W., 23)

Such talk might have seemed like little more than the bravado of a frustrated adolescent, were it not for what followed.

REBELLION AND ITS AFTERMATH

Al-Mutanabbi's sobriquet, meaning "the would-be prophet" or "one who claims prophethood," originates from the events that took place in his life in Syria around 934 CE. There is no unanimity, among either Arab scholars or westerners, as to whether al-Mutanabbi actually claimed to be a prophet. In Islamic societies that believe in the Qur'anic declaration that Muhammad is the seal of the prophets (33:40), the question is a serious one. Accordingly, many modern Arab commentators, in an attempt to defend their poet against charges of unbelief, reject the idea out of hand. Despite the lingering questions about al-Mutanabbi's claims and whether or not he believed them himself, the outline of the ensuing events is reasonably clear.

During his third visit to the city of Latakia, al-Mutanabbi apparently became acquainted with Abu 'Abd Allah Mu'adh ibn Isma'il, to whom he declared himself a prophet. He claimed as proof a text similar to the Qur'an consisting, like the sacred text, of 114 chapters, which constituted a direct challenge to the Muslim belief in the inimitability of the Qur'anic text. As further proof, al-Mutanabbi is said to have contrived petty miracles, such as stopping rain in a specific area while the surrounding region was being doused. We have no further details about the substantive nature of the poet's claims. A number of scholars consider them to have been Qarmatian in origin, while Wolfhart Heinrichs has made an interesting case for a connection with the gnostic Shi'ite groups active in the area at the time (Heinrichs, 1990, 125). Al-Mutanabbi himself, when later asked whether or not he had claimed prophethood, defended himself in a number of ways. His name, "the would-be prophet," he said, had nothing to do with any behavior on his part, but rather had been given to him by others on the basis of specific verses of his poetry that seemed to make such claims, such as verses 18 and 36 of a poem written for an unknown patron:

> My stay in the abode of Nakhlah
> is like nothing if not the sojourn of the Messiah among the Jews.
>
> (W., 32)
>
> I am among a people – may God overtake them –
> a stranger, like Salih among Thamud.
>
> (W., 35)

The latter, which refers to the pre-Islamic prophet Salih, mentioned in the Qur'an, who was rejected by the people he was sent to warn (7:73–79; 11:61–68; 26:141–59; 27:45–53), was particularly cited. Another response al-Mutanabbi frequently gave to disavow the sobriquet and the claims it implied was to furnish an alternative etymology for the name, claiming that it was derived from roots meaning "elevation" and "exaltedness" and had nothing to do with claiming prophethood. On at least one occasion, though, the poet offered an oblique acknowledgement of the affair by referring to it as having been caused by "childishness in his youth."

Shortly after his encounter with Mu'adh, after his fame had spread among the Bedouin, al-Mutanabbi led the tribes of the Samawah region of the Syrian desert in a series of raids. Later, the disruptions expanded to Salamiyyah, northeast of the Syrian city of Hums. Finally, the Ikhshidid-appointed governor of Hums, Lu'lu' al-Ghuri, sent out an army against the tribes, and al-Mutanabbi was captured. He spent two years (934–936) in prison, and was released only after a jailer took pity on the now gravely ill man and transmitted a poetic appeal from him to the new governor, Ishaq Ibn Kayghulugh. An influential figure seems also to have interceded on his behalf, and the poet had to agree to a public recanting of his crime of heresy.

The information available makes it difficult to determine what precise combination of religious rebellion, political ambition, and plain old greed was at the heart of al-Mutanabbi's ill-fated activities, but it is clear that at least the latter two remained stable features of his personality. During his life, despite his lofty declarations about the baseness of greed, so in keeping with the Arab tradition, al-Mutanabbi became infamous for his materialistic and acquisitive nature. And he never ceased his attachment to the grandiose image of himself as a great hero, reflected in some of the verses cited above. The Bedouins' readiness to engage in raiding during his short-lived rebellion offered the poet the opportunity to sate at least these two needs – on the one hand, for spoils, and on the other, for the adventure and glory of battle. What religious or philosophical basis he actually offered for this behavior remains unclear.

AFTER THE FALL

After his release from prison, al-Mutanabbi once more became an itinerant panegyrist for petty princes and unknown patrons; for example, he composed a number of poems for chancellery and customs secretaries. This is not surprising: during the 'Abbasid era, secretaries had become important patrons of literature and arbiters of taste; some were themselves poets of merit.

Understandably, the poems of this period do not have the rebellious voice of the pre-prison pieces. It is not true, however, as some scholars have suggested, that al-Mutanabbi's personality virtually disappeared from his work, now that he was on good behavior in the hope of attracting a worthy and reliable patron. Al-Mutanabbi was constitutionally incapable of completely sanitizing his poetry of his own voice. In some accounts of the poet's career, al-Mutanabbi's art is described almost as a consolation prize, which he settled for once he had failed at his attempt to conquer the world. The converse is just as likely. It is impossible to know, but we must wonder whether al-Mutanabbi would ever have turned into the marauding rebel who landed up in prison, if his poetry had initially met with the kind of reception he expected. Given the repeated references in his early poetry to the goal of acquiring wealth and the difficulty of doing so, it seems that material gain was the poet's overriding concern.

As we will see in the next chapter, al-Mutanabbi was well able to sublimate whatever warrior hero image he had of himself when he was in the employ of Sayf al-Dawlah. During that time al-Mutanabbi, close associate of a leader who fit the poet's vision of heroic Arab ruler, was able to turn his poetry itself into the field of glory that his heroic aspirations demanded. In the *pas de deux* that was the poet – patron relationship, it was enough for Sayf al-Dawlah to play the grand warrior and benefactor, and have it instantiated in verse by al-Mutanabbi.

AT KHARSHANI'S COURT

Around the end of 939, al-Mutanabbi came as close as he ever had to grabbing the brass ring of patronage. He became the official poet of Badr ibn 'Ammar ibn Isma'il al-Kharshani, governor of the town of Tiberias in Syria. This was the first time that al-Mutanabbi got to taste the kind of luxury that sustained and generous sponsorship could provide. At the same time, it was his most profound experience thus far of the rigors of court life, including the inevitable wine drinking and the demand to compose poetry extemporaneously. Though he hated it, al-Mutanabbi sometimes did drink, and he even occasionally extemporized while under the influence of alcohol. But spontaneous verse was not al-Mutanabbi's forte, and detractors who wished to undermine his position at court were quick to suggest that his extemporized verse had been prepared in advance. So, while al-Mutanabbi was definitely getting a taste of the good life, and his reputation as a poet was growing, he was also living under the strain of a court society that he did not take to easily. Ultimately, his enemies at court took advantage of his absence from a trip Badr made to the coast of Syria to change the governor's opinion of the poet, and, as a result of this change of heart, al-Mutanabbi was forced to flee Badr's court after slightly more than a year of service.

Al-Mutanabbi sought refuge with a friend, but when the governor pursued him he had to flee to the desert and live among the Bedouin. His anger, sadness, and frustration at being back where he had started, only now being pursued by a powerful governor, is clear from the poems composed at this time. The poems composed for Badr al-Kharshani had been fairly traditional in style and free of the bombast of the earlier period, but the tone of the poems composed after their falling out is reminiscent of the pre-revolt works. Once more, as if his innate superiority and nobility accounted for his limited professional success, he describes himself as being above base greed and bogus ambition:

> He who envies the contemptible for his way of life is [himself] debased, many are the lifestyles to which death is preferable.
>
> (W., 245)

DEATH OF THE POET'S GRANDMOTHER

Badr's departure for Baghdad meant al-Mutanabbi was able to return to the cities of Syria, where once again he composed poetry for diverse notables of modest rank. Probably at the beginning of 941, around the time he became associated with a young judge, Muhammad ibn 'Abd Allah al-Khasibi, al-Mutanabbi received news of the death of his beloved grandmother. In the poem he composed on this occasion, al-Mutanabbi re-shapes the traditional poetic mode of elegy and makes it a dynamic space in which the poet's sense of his own greatness becomes the vehicle for his recovery from grief. In this piece, pre-Islamic values are present as points of contrast with the novel stance the poet assumes. From the very beginning, al-Mutanabbi declines to blame fate for the horrible occurrence, for its "violence is not impetuousness and [its] refraining [from it] is not restraint." In other words, fate, the catch-all explanation in the pre-Islamic poetic universe, is not a human agent, making choices for which it might be held responsible. The natural human response to the death of a loved one is to try to explain the unexplainable and to fix responsibility; in this case, the only potentially blameworthy person in the picture is the poet, who left his grandmother to go and seek his fortune, and over the course of the poem al-Mutanabbi comes to terms with the choices he has made. In the poem, the person of the poet merges with that of the deceased, eventually to supplant her as its main topic. Both the dead woman and the poet are associated with the beloved of the Arab literary tradition and the various configurations of separation/death they each experienced are evoked. The grandmother died of the pain of separation, and the poet experienced a foretaste of her death, which he had always feared, in the separation from her, and then, metaphorically, died of grief over her. Alternatively, the grandmother died of happiness at receiving a letter from her grandson. In either case, the poet is at the source of it all. Worldly man that he is, he knew how cruel fate can be and yet still he left to make his mark in the world. The poet provides a miniature narrative, in which the scene of his grandmother jubilantly receiving a letter from him is vividly painted:

> She marvels at my handwriting and my words
> as if she is seeing in the lines of letters white-winged ravens
> And she kisses it until its ink has turned
> the area around her eyes and her teeth black.
>
> (W., 261)

The immediacy of this scene is conveyed by the series of imperfect tense verbs it employs until it is abruptly ended by the intrusion of death, via the definitive perfect tense:

> Her tears stopped flowing and her eyelids dried
> and her love for me left her heart after having wounded it.
>
> (W., 261)

This manipulation of verb tense to create a sense of evolving narrative features even in some of al-Mutanabbi's very early poems. Al-Mutanabbi never developed this technique so well as his predecessor, Abu Nuwas, though he did sometimes employ it effectively, as in this example, to produce a sense of vitality that the conventional forms seemed to militate against.

In a magnificently ironic line (verse 16), the poet expresses the essential paradox of life: "Here I am seeking water from the clouds for her grave / when I used to seek to water the battle and the hard spears" (W., 262). He has wound up in the passive position of praying that it will rain upon his grandmother's grave, when he once actively watered the battlefield with the blood of his enemies. The situations in the two hemistichs of this verse describe the profound contrast between the powerlessness of the bereaved in the face of death and the power of the warrior who presumes to determine life and death in battle. The bereaved poet, once so bold and mighty, is now immobilized, powerless to take vengeance on the fever that caused his grandmother's death. After a cathartic eruption of grief and emotion, the poet reconstitutes himself in an extended boast that concludes the poem.

Boasting of the noble lineage of the deceased is a standard feature of pre-Islamic and post-Islamic elegy. What is noteworthy here is that, according to the poet, it is not tribal affiliation that is the source of his grandmother's excellence, but rather her association with him and the fact that she engendered someone as great as he:

> Even if you weren't the daughter of the most noble father
> your magnificent lineage would be your being a mother to me
> If the evil-wishers' day was made pleasant by her death
> she has [still] engendered through me a vexation they must bear.
>
> (W., 263)

He concludes with the ultimate expression of bravado, in which he prefers death to a life without honor:

> This is the way I am, world, depart if you wish
> And, oh soul, keep pursuing the things it (i.e., the world) despises

> May an hour not pass for me that does not honor me
> and may a soul that accepts oppression not abide with me.
>
> (W., 264)

Al-Mutanabbi is here explicitly replacing the pre-Islamic emphasis on communal values and identity with a focus on individual distinction. Indeed this is the spirit of the entire poem. From the very first line, the pre-Islamic emphasis on fate is rejected, to be replaced by the individual's assumption of existential responsibility. In this poem, the process is configured by the stages of grieving that are at the heart of the piece, but on a larger level this is also what is going on in much of al-Mutanabbi's *oeuvre*. Al-Mutanabbi took great pride in his own tribal heritage, but for him it was just one ingredient, albeit an important one, in the sense of self and of individual worth to which he was primarily attached. In this elegy, al-Mutanabbi is articulating a new ethic for a new age, using the terms set by the old edifice.

THE IKHSHIDID CONNECTION

By the end of 941, al-Mutanabbi, frustrated with the insecurity and the modesty of his circumstances, put aside his aversion to panegyrizing non-Arab rulers, and set his sights on the court of Muhammad al-Ikhshid, who had regained control over much of Syria. He composed a number of panegyrics in honor of figures associated with al-Ikhshid, including the captain of his navy, in the hope of gaining an entrée to his court. His efforts were successful; al-Mutanabbi recited for al-Ikhshid, was rewarded generously, and was appointed his official panegyrist. As luck – or the lack of it – would have it, Muhammad al-Ikhshid died shortly after this appointment and the newly minted court poet was passed on to his young son. When it became clear that the actual ruler was the regent, Kafur, al-Mutanabbi could not bring himself to praise this non-Arab black eunuch, and, further urged to action by an assassination attempt, left the Ikhshidid court. His next patron was the nephew of Muhammad al-Ikhshid, Abu Muhammad al-Hasan ibn 'Ubayd Allah, the youthful governor of Ramlah in Palestine. Al-Mutanabbi acknowledged that his brief stay at the court of Ramlah was a turning point for him. Not only was he generously paid for his poetry, but for the first time he felt that he was receiving the respect that he deserved, both from the governor, and from members of his administration, who received him as a dignitary in their own courts.

EYE ON THE HAMDANID PRIZE

Al-Mutanabbi's ambition would not let him rest on his laurels, and his Arab pride yearned for a kindred spirit as patron. After several months of tranquility and security, al-Mutanabbi left Ramlah with the goal of establishing a connection with the Hamdanid ruler of Aleppo, Sayf al-Dawlah. Early in his career, al-Mutanabbi had made two unsuccessful attempts to make contact with him; this time he decided to employ a go-between and headed for the court of Sayf al-Dawlah's cousin, Abu 'l-'Asha'ir, the governor of Antioch. While passing through Tripoli, he had the misfortune to cross paths with his former jailer, and when Ishaq Ibn Kayghulugh, now governor of that city, requested that al-Mutanabbi compose a panegyric for him, the poet was not forthcoming. It is a clear measure of the respect al-Mutanabbi had garnered, and of his stature as a poet, that he did not relent, even when the governor forcibly prevented him from continuing on his way. Al-Mutanabbi may not initially have had the wisdom to understand that creating a reputation would be a long and at times ungratifying process, but despite his youthful impatience and his insistent pride, he had emerged from those early, frustrating, years to become a respected and sought-after panegyrist. And he knew it.

Al-Mutanabbi was keenly aware of the market for his poetry, and one stylistic feature of his work suggests that his vision of his potential audience was quite wide. One of the prized characteristics of Arabic poetry was the quotability of individual verses. Even medieval critics, who had the expertise and wherewithal to discuss entire poems, tended to focus on discrete verses. The prevailing structure of poetry, with its emphasis on self-contained verses, each supposed to convey a complete thought, encouraged this focus on the individual line. The emphasis on memorizing in Arab culture further guaranteed that aficionados would focus on outstanding individual verses and repeat them in other arenas, spreading the fame of their author. During this early stage of his career, al-Mutanabbi's attention to the conciseness of his verses became increasingly more pronounced. Many of his pithy verse sayings which have become part and parcel of the common parlance were coined during this time, and it is not unlikely that the poet himself had an astute eye for precisely this kind of popularity.

Al-Mutanabbi managed to escape the virtual house arrest Ishaq ibn Kayghulugh had imposed on him, but before leaving Tripoli he composed a bitter invective against the governor and entrusted it to a friend, with instructions that it be disseminated once the poet was out of harm's way.

He had started to learn how to reconcile the demands of his profession as panegyrist with the needs of his vast ego and insistent personality. His lyrical musings about the paradoxes of life and his existential angst often provided the framework of his poems, but, unlike in his formative years, did not distract him from the demands of both convention and his clients. It is partly his ability to combine the two that make his poetry so compelling. In a poetic environment that had limited space for a personal presence, al-Mutanabbi laid claim to a corner of the traditional landscape for his individual voice, thereby transforming the very nature of those traditions. At the ripe old age of thirty-three, al-Mutanabbi was an established panegyrist, but had yet to reach the peak of either his professional success or his creative influence. For that, he required a subject with some semblance of the true Arab hero that abode in his imagination. This he was to find in the person of his greatest patron, the Hamdanid prince, Sayf al-Dawlah.

3

GLORY DAYS IN ALEPPO

THE HAMDANIDS OF ALEPPO

Into the vacuum left by the disintegration of 'Abbasid power stepped a number of rulers of provincial principalities. In most cases, neither the sphere of influence nor the ambitions of these petty governments extended beyond their limited geographical areas and their local inhabitants, but the Hamdanids of Aleppo were a somewhat different case.

The Aleppan branch of the Hamdanid dynasty was led by the younger of the two founding brothers, 'Ali ibn Abi'l-Hayja', dubbed "Sayf al-Dawlah" (the sword of the state) by the 'Abbasid caliph, in recognition of his military triumphs on behalf of the 'Abbasids. Like many other local princes, the Hamdanids had used their service in the caliph's army as a stepping-stone to their own independent principality. Unlike his older brother, who was preoccupied with protecting the Iraqi end of the family dynasty in Mosul, Sayf al-Dawlah assumed a grand leadership role, attempting to stem the Byzantine military resurgence, and thereby taking up the job the enervated caliph was no longer able to perform. His offensive raids into Byzantine territory, along with severe fiscal policies and confiscations of agricultural land, provided an abundant income to support the brilliant and opulent court for which he became famous.

Sayf al-Dawlah placed local authority over his territories in the hands of trusted family members and friends, so the court of Aleppo undertook only limited administration and was free to luxuriate in its vibrant intellectual and social life, reigned over personally by Sayf al-Dawlah, a man of great learning. In addition to formal assemblies, Sayf al-Dawlah held smaller gatherings, rather like literary *salons*. These provided opportunities for more casual interaction and greater intimacy between the prince and the members of his inner circle. Even in these gatherings, debate was lively and the jockeying for favor constant, with the result that numerous rivalries developed among the prince's intimates and protégés. Al-Mutanabbi had to be constantly on his toes, prepared to hold his own against grammarians, other poets, and scholars from diverse fields. Thinkers, and intellectuals of all types, were sponsored at Sayf al-Dawlah's court: theologians, philosophers, philologists, astronomers, and poets. Among the renowned scholars that graced the Hamdanid's assemblies were the philosopher, al-Farabi, the philologist, Ibn Khalawayh, and the poet, Abu Firas al-Hamdani, cousin of Sayf al-Dawlah. The latter two were to be perpetual thorns in al-Mutanabbi's side during his nine years at the court of Aleppo.

Despite the pressure to perform, for al-Mutanabbi these were the best of days. A self-fashioned champion of Islam, Sayf al-Dawlah had passion and bravery, alas, not always matched by tactical shrewdness, that had helped raise him to the status of hero in the minds of many. He had a certain impetuous flair and grandiosity that were expressed not only on the battlefield but also in his brilliant court. An ambitious Muslim and proud member of the Arab tribe of Taghlib, Sayf al-Dawlah was keenly attached to the traditional Arab values that al-Mutanabbi also admired: for example, Sayf al-Dawlah spent a great deal of money on ransoms for Muslims captured during battle. Though capable of great severity, he often tempered his behavior and showed compassion towards members of the Arab tribes he routed. At a minimum, all this would have made the demeaning role of paid panegyrist at least palatable to al-Mutanabbi, but it did much more, and al-Mutanabbi's poetry in honor of Sayf al-Dawlah often conveys an unmistakable respect and affection for his Hamdanid patron.

AL-MUTANABBI'S FIRST ODE TO SAYF AL-DAWLAH

Al-Mutanabbi's days as the paid poet of Abu'l-'Asha'ir, the governor of Antioch, a position that would have satisfied many an ambitious panegyrist, were a mere stepping-stone to the greater prize of the governor's cousin, Sayf al-Dawlah. When, fresh from new military victories, Sayf al-Dawlah made a triumphal visit to Antioch, al-Mutanabbi, thanks to the intercession of Abu'l-'Asha'ir, had the opportunity to recite his poetry for him for the first time. Of the three poems composed for Sayf al-Dawlah during his stay at his cousin's court, only the first was a polythematic ode; the others were occasional poems – "occasional" in both the sense that they treated only one topic and the sense that they were occasioned by the particular circumstances of the moment. Sayf al-Dawlah had decided to leave Antioch and return to Aleppo, and in two short poems al-Mutanabbi appealed to him to change his plans and stay on.

Only a fully fledged, formal, polythematic ode celebrating the victories of the conquering hero would have sufficient ceremonial grandeur to display al-Mutanabbi's skills and impress the would-be patron. Accordingly, the poem al-Mutanabbi produced ("Your faithfulness is like the abode ...") contained the conventional amatory prelude, including a departure scene in which the beloved is described riding in her litter on the back of a white camel. This initial section is punctuated by philosophical declarations about life and the vicissitudes of fate, along the lines of his elegy to his grandmother. After a brief stylized description of the travails the poet had endured to reach the patron, the hero is lauded in the panegyric section of the poem for his bravery, his generosity, and his nobility of spirit. This is all completely conventional: Blachère describes this piece as "strained" (1935, 148); I would call it careful. At this point, al-Mutanabbi barely knows the prince. He would have heard of his great learning and passion for literature and known of his brilliant court, but they did not yet have a personal relationship and he could not afford to take too many chances. Therefore, in this ode, unlike in many others, the poet's personality takes a back seat. Despite this understandable caution, the poem provides not only clear previews of coming poetic attractions, but also some noteworthy manipulations of conventional poetic motifs.

In the very first line of the poem, al-Mutanabbi invokes the traditional motif of crying over the deserted abode of the beloved, including reference to the two companions often called on to share the poet's misery. However, the two companions, who are directly addressed, are presented as failing to fulfill their obligation, as friends, to cry with the poet and thus help ease the pain of his loss: "Your faithfulness is like the abode, the saddest part of it that which is effaced, / while the most healing of tears are those that flow" (W., 373). In al-Mutanabbi's formulation the two friends become a source of further sadness for the poet, and he finds himself having to defend his insistent need to shed copious tears. This obviously serves to exaggerate the pathos of the traditional opening: the poet is aggrieved not only by the loss of his beloved, but also by the disappointing behavior of his friends. He is doubly abandoned. More importantly, it emphasizes the existential aloneness of the poet, and the grief and sadness he experiences are emphatically represented as the experience of an individual rather than a group or implied community. This is reinforced by the succeeding line, in which al-Mutanabbi presents the forsaken lover as being not only abandoned but also harassed by his critics. Not only do his erstwhile friends not lament with him; they also find fault with his need to weep:

> I am aught but a lover and for every lover
> the most derelict of his two pure friends is the one who blames him.
>
> (W., 374)

It is interesting to note that al-Mutanabbi merges a pre-Islamic motif – the crying with two companions over the abandoned abode – with a feature (the censurers who criticize the lover's behavior) most commonly found in 'Abbasid love poetry. The companions of the pre-Islamic tradition are transformed into the killjoys of 'Abbasid love poetry. As is often his wont, in line 3 al-Mutanabbi generalizes the experience into a universally applicable dictum:

Other than the [true] people of love may take on the cloak of love
and a person may seek friendship from those who are not appropriate
to him.

(W., 374)

In this way, the poet succeeds in presenting himself as the defiant lover who stubbornly adheres to his attachment in the face of abandonment and censure; a stance he spells out explicitly in the next two lines (4 and 5). Al-Mutanabbi was roundly criticized, by even some of his staunchest supporters, for what many deemed the bad taste of line 4:

May I be worn down like the remains if I do not halt
by them as would a miser whose ring has been lost in the dirt,
depressed. So let those who censure love beware me
as the trainer of refractory horses is wary of them.

(W., 374–375)

The significance of this stance of individual persistence on the part of the lover comes to the fore as the poet, as is frequently done in 'Abbasid poetry, conflates the beloved of the traditional amatory prelude with the patron who is the recipient of the poem. This is made possible because in Arabic poetry the beloved, whether female or male, may be referred to by grammatical terms that are masculine in gender. The opening few lines of this prelude are followed by a completely conventional departure scene, in which the poet depicts his beloved leaving with her tribe, riding in a litter carried on the back of a camel. The women in the litter are described as blossoms, the curtains of the howdahs their calyxes. The beloved's companions, travelling with her in the dark, have no need for the moon, so brilliant is her light. In all of this the poet uses feminine referents; indeed, the scene commences with an explicit imperative, unmistakably feminine in form: "Stop, so that the first glance can redeem my soul/with a second one, for whosoever spoils something must pay for it" (W., 376). Then, in line 10, the poet shifts to the masculine, in a verse that could be understood as referring either to the beloved or to the patron he is trying to woo: "A beloved, as if beauty was in love with him / and so gave preference to him, or [as if] the one distributing beauty had acted unfairly" (W., 377). This grammatical structure itself, where the subject ("she is" or "he is") is omitted from explicit expression, emphasizes the blurring of the distinction between the mythic beloved of the poetic tradition and the object of the poet's praise and his potential sponsor, Sayf al-Dawlah. The next two lines of praise alternate between terms referring to the male world of war and clear references to the female beloved. The transition between the two is accomplished by applying terms more properly part of one world to the other. For example, in verse 12 ("The dust of the horses becomes the nearest of her curtains / while the farthest is the aroma of the incense clinging to her" (W., 377), the phrase "the dust of the horses" is plucked from its usual environment – the description of battle scenes – and applied to the concluding frame of the beloved's departure.

The effect of all this is multi-layered. It serves to exaggerate the poet's promised devotion to and reverence for the potential patron. More potently, it serves to fold the patron – his grandeur and the awe he inspires in others – into the powerful mythic *Gestalt* of the traditional poetic motif. Calling this simply a manneristic technique would minimize the emotional effect it has in the poem. In the pre-Islamic poetic universe, weeping over the remains of a beloved's abode is a uniquely powerful motif in that it goes to the heart of the basic human need for connection, made all the more poignant by the changeable nature of the desert environment from which the poetry emanates. What attachment means for the individual's sense of himself in the face of the fleetingness of life and love, and how he deals with the experience of loss, that is the essense of the amatory prelude. Incorporating the patron into that profound emotional experience from the poetic tradition not only lends him a measure of its historical and symbolic power as the well-spring of the Arab poetic tradition, but also puts him at the heart of the most primary human experience. This is especially so in this poem, since the poet-lover has stripped himself of other human connection and comfort and presented himself as utterly alone in the world, and thus all the more in need of Sayf al-Dawlah's attention. On a more pragmatic level, the poet's neediness is emphasized, so that when, later in the piece, he appeals to Sayf al-Dawlah for generous reward, his claims seem much more pressing.

One of the features of this poem that has attracted some attention is the extended description of the tent in which Sayf al-Dawlah received visitors during his time in Antioch. As Blachère noted, and as we can observe in a number of other poems by al-Mutanabbi, the poet was obviously exploiting this topic as a means of inserting some novelty into the conventional fare of the ode. The poet was not yet an intimate of Sayf al-Dawlah; he had not yet accompanied him in battle and did not have details of any military campaigns to focus on in his poem. Still, this effort at creating some variation is far more dynamic than Blachère's description suggests.

Al-Mutanabbi describes the scenes depicted on the embroidered material of the tent's walls, which include "gardens that no cloud has woven" and tree branches "whose doves do not sing" (W., 379). "When the wind strikes it, it undulates as if/its old horses are ambling about and its lions are stalking their prey" (W., 379). Most importantly, the Byzantine king is pictured submissively bowing down to kiss the ground before the Arab prince. One of the effects of this little ekphrastic excursion is to draw attention to the very act of representing and particularly to al-Mutanabbi's cleverness at it. Al-Mutanabbi is here finding a new angle to the mannerism of prevailing poetic taste. Like an infolding arabesque, poetry of the period was heavily self-reflexive, drawing attention to its own language and clever conceits. By focusing on the pictorial representations on the tent's walls, al-Mutanabbi takes this preoccupation with representation one degree further. The irony – and indeed the genius – is that by concentrating on an object at an even greater representational distance from the real-life Sayf al-Dawlah and his court than the poem being recited, al-Mutanabbi infuses the recitation scene, and hence his poem, with new life and loosens the fetters of manneristic self-reflection. In contrast to the stylized images embroidered on the fabric of the tent walls, the poet's composition takes on a new ring of truth. It is easier to appreciate the effect of this mechanism if we imagine the setting in which the poem was delivered and realize that this was not so much a recitation as a performance in which the hackneyed pursuit of eulogy for a brave ruler is given new blood, and the image of the heroic Sayf al-Dawlah, foregrounded against the blur of inferior imitations, stands out clearly and emphatically.

To justify his appeal to Sayf al-Dawlah for a generous reward, the poet describes the difficulties he has endured to reach the prince and praises him for his liberality. He has crossed "deserts where the wolf's soul would not accompany him/nor would the raven's forefeathers carry him" (W., 382). His arrogance in check, al-Mutanabbi then touches on a theme that would become a constant refrain in his poetry to Sayf al-Dawlah: that only he, al-Mutanabbi, was a great enough poet to do justice to Sayf al-Dawlah's merits. All the other poets were mere babblers, whose skills were not up to the task of describing so magnificent a hero:

> I was upset for him when I saw his attributes
> without a describer, while the inarticulate babble poetry.
>
> (W., 382)

At various points throughout this poem, the poet borrows from the vocabulary and typology of classic Arabic love poetry. The poet is represented as devoted lover and emphasis is placed on hidden enemies and the concealment and/or divulging of secrets and signs. His description of the pitch-black darkness of the lonely journey he endured to reach Sayf al-Dawlah is one example:

> When I made up my mind to head for a distant land
> I walked at night, I the secret and the night the one keeping it.
>
> (W., 382)

The flavor of the pre-Islamic "outlaw" poets' descriptions of solitary walking in the desert is clearly discernible here.

Finally, al-Mutanabbi employs a conceit that he repeatedly used in his days in Aleppo: playing on the title of his patron (which literally means "sword of the state") when he exclaims in verse 37: "Glory has drawn the sword of the state" (W., 382). He emphasizes the supportive role Sayf al-Dawlah has played for the 'Abbasid caliph, but then, distinguishing between his given name and this title bestowed on him by the caliph, makes bold to intimate that Sayf al-Dawlah is, in truth, his superior. This is a theme that he would take up even more forthrightly in a later poem:

> His sword suspender is on the shoulder of the noble caliph
> and the hilt of his sword is in the hand of the Almighty of the heavens
> ...
> The one who named [him] Ali was indeed just,
> while the one who called him Sayf did him an injustice.
>
> (W., 382; 383)

Line 42 specifies why the title "Sayf al-Dawlah" is inadequate for the prince: "The point of every sword does not cut the head [of the enemy]/ but his noble deeds cut off the calamities of time" (W., 383), but the implication that Sayf al-Dawlah, namesake of the assassinated fourth "orthodox" caliph (considered the rightful successor to the Prophet Muhammad in the eyes of the "party of 'Ali"), was meant for a grander position of authority would not have been missed by his Shi'ite audience.

OCCASIONAL POEMS FOR THE WOULD-BE PATRON

Al-Mutanabbi followed this composition with two shorter ones ("Where have you resolved [to go] ..." [W., 383] and "Go easy, lofty prince ..." [W., 386]), which urged Sayf al-Dawlah to prolong his stay in Antioch. Although the stakes were fairly high for al-Mutanabbi, the brevity and hyper-conventionality of the first of these two poems suggest a more casual performance setting than that of the ode.

There is nothing very original about either of these two pieces. The second, more interesting, poem ("Go easy, lofty prince ...") conveys, in a particularly clear manner, the constraints on the late

'Abbasid poet – especially when he was trying, as al-Mutanabbi was, to impress a potential "maecenas."

Creatively, the panegyrist of the tenth century was in a very difficult situation. His job was to praise his subject, but the grounds for adulation had already been firmly established by culture. The patron was brave, generous, and the best of all possible rulers; his lineage was impressive, and his character noble. This was the required content of a praise poem. The only question for the poet was how to say, in a somewhat new way, what hundreds of poets before him had said. Without details born of intimacy, or a particular context, any poet would be hard-pressed to make his poetry stand out. Clever metaphors, such as the one in verse 18 of al-Mutanabbi's first ode to Sayf al-Dawlah ("Your faithfulness is like the abode ..."), were a staple of the ongoing quest for originality:

> Better [even] than all the juice of youth
> is the rain of a lightning cloud in a tent, which I look to as if forecasting rain by the clouds

(W., 379)

In the poem "Go easy, lofty prince ...", as in others, the strain of traditional expectation shows when al-Mutanabbi's hyperbole results in ludicrous verses such as: "Every noble lord's scalp wishes that/its part were the path of your passage." (W., 387)

What the poet basically wants to say to Sayf al-Dawlah is: don't leave; it's raining too much. The mention of rain immediately leads the poet to the conventional likening of the patron to the clouds, and his generosity to the abundant rain. So bountiful are the clouds that the poet wonders if they belong to the tribe of Taghlib, Sayf al-Dawlah's tribe. He then uses a logical implication of his urging a change in the prince's plan as the jumping-off point for a series of verses lauding Sayf al-Dawlah's bravery: don't for a minute think that I'm encouraging you to wait out the rain because you cannot handle the rigors of travel in inclement weather, he says; on the contrary: "If a young man is accustomed to facing down death [on the battlefield]/then mud is the least thing he might experience" (W., 387).

The water of the flooded valleys the prince might travel is likened to the enemy blood he has made run in their ravines. The rough ground along his way will surely yield to one who has taken over fortresses and found no resistance. Al-Mutanabbi thus found a logical hook that opened up a way for him to say what everyone knew he had to say. This small turn of thought, the clever use of details of the moment, gives this poem its appeal. The ability to seize on details, whether of logic or circumstance, as the point of departure for his poems is one of the skills that helped al-Mutanabbi navigate his way around the conventional limitations of his day.

This poem, like the foregoing ones, contains a number of verses imitative of lines composed by well-known predecessors. Summoning up the poetry of earlier poets was inevitable, and even desirable, in a culture in which poetry was primarily a communal experience. The audience wanted, and expected, to be able to recognize the ideas, even the partial quoting, of precedents in any given poem, because a large part of the pleasure of poetry was in the communal celebration of the shared literary heritage. The skilled poet's difficult task was to find a delicate balance between celebration of the tradition and innovation. Al-Mutanabbi's evocation of the poetry of ancient (pre-Islamic) and modern ('Abbasid) poets would have impressed on Sayf al-Dawlah the extent of his mastery of the poetic canon. Judging from the outcome of these first recitations, it seems that, in the eyes of Sayf al-Dawlah, al-Mutanabbi had also managed to come up with enough that was novel.

DEATH OF SAYF AL-DAWLAH'S MOTHER

Al-Mutanabbi did not accompany Sayf al-Dawlah when he left Antioch. In the view of Mahmud Shakir, the reason was the ill health of al-Mutanabbi's pregnant wife, who later died, following a difficult birth (Shakir, 1978, 208). Shakir's is one of the few attempts to explain, on the basis of his life experiences, the pessimism that pervades al-Mutanabbi's poetry. But by December 948 the poet had joined his new patron in Aleppo and there recited to him an elegy on the latter's recently deceased mother.

As in the first ode to Sayf al-Dawlah ("Your faithfulness is like the abode ..."), al-Mutanabbi puts the vocabulary of love poetry to work in a new environment. In the earlier poem, this enabled al-Mutanabbi to inject emotional power into the formal and predictable panegyric ode and exaggerate the psychological importance of Sayf al-Dawlah and the poet's devotion to him. In the elegy on Sayf al-Dawlah's mother ("We make ready swords and lances ..."), this vocabulary is employed not only to enrich the portrayal of the deceased in a similar fashion, but also to underline the essential paradox of death. The poet emphasizes the finality and completeness of the separation from the beloved woman in verses that resonate with the traditional amatory prelude of an ode, which, in keeping with poetic custom, is technically absent from this elegiac poem.

> In spite of us you have descended to a place
> where you are far from the south wind and the north
> The scent of lavender is veiled from you,
> and the dews of the showers are barred from you
> In an abode whose every inhabitant is a stranger
> long absent, all ties broken.
>
> (W., 392)

The deceased woman is praised for being chaste, sheltered in life as she now is in her grave:

> May the blessings of God, our Creator, be the perfume
> upon the face shrouded in beauty,
> Upon one who, out of chastity, was buried before [being buried] in the dust
> and [entombed] in noble qualities before the tomb.
>
> How many an eye [once] covered in kisses
> now wears mascara of stone and sand?
>
> (W., 390; 393)

Al-Mutanabbi's choice of metaphors is significant. As Andras Hamori so eloquently put it, the deceased wears "the cosmetic of the grave and the winding sheet of loveliness.... [M]etaphors of this kind move back and forth between life and death, easily and evenly as sinister pendulums," and "blur the comforting boundary line between the two states" (Hamori, 1974, 140).

It is not just the departed woman with whom union is impossible, but the world – and life – itself. Sayf al-Dawlah's dead mother is like an unattainable lover, but so too is the world. Humans enjoy a brief taste of life, but ultimately possess no control over it and have no power over its coming and going.

> Who has not loved this world from of old?
> But there is no path to union.
> Your share of the beloved during your lifetime
> is like your share of a phantom during your sleep.
>
> (W., 388–89)

It is standard, in early Arabic elegy, to praise the deceased person and the surviving members of her tribe. Relatives who have attained some renown in battle and society are thus amply lauded. The mention of the deceased's attributes and the celebration of their survivors' merits soften the reality of loss. In this poem, therefore, al-Mutanabbi would be expected to praise Sayf al-Dawlah as a statesman and warrior. It is thus striking that the poet begins the elegy with a stark statement of the ultimate human dilemma of mortality which forthrightly acknowledges the limits of the military mastery regularly attributed to Sayf al-Dawlah, the son of the deceased woman:

> We make ready swords and lances
> and death slays us without a battle;
> we station the swift steeds near our tents,
> but they do not deliver from the ambling of the nights.
>
> (W., 388)

In a sense, this acknowledgement of the human condition renders the laudatory description of Sayf al-Dawlah at the end of the poem all the more heroic – in an existential, true sense that is rare in classical

Arabic poetry. Sayf al-Dawlah is all the braver *because* of the inherent limits of his power. Fate is perfidious and death takes on many forms, but in the face of this changeability Sayf al-Dawlah is the reliable, consistent rock:

> O Sayf al-Dawlah, seek succor in fortitude –
> and how could the mountains [ever] equal your fortitude?
> You teach mankind how to bear patiently
> and how to plunge into death in unpredictable war.
> The circumstances of fate that you face are varied,
> but your state is one in every condition.

(W., 394)

This poem thus represents a deft combination of traditional generic expectations with a philosophical stance that provides depth to the familiar poetic mode. By applying the vocabulary of love poetry to the elegy, al-Mutanabbi focuses the poem's attention on the inherent irony of life and the fact that the permanence of life and love is not commensurate with our attachment to them.

ELEGY ON ABU'L-HAYJA'

Sayf al-Dawlah was apparently a man quite devoted to his family. The elegy on his mother was the first of six that al-Mutanabbi would compose in honor of members of that family. Coming, as it did, so early in their association, it must have cemented the budding relationship between the two men. On the occasion of the even greater tragedy of the death of Sayf al-Dawlah's infant son, in 949, less than a year after the death of his mother, al-Mutanabbi composed an elegy ("Because of you, we, above the ground …") that is at once stark lament, moral guidance, philosophical brooding, and praise for the patron-employer. Al-Mutanabbi not only evokes the traditional motifs of Arabic elegy, but also of the polythematic ode, ultimately to have them nullified by overwhelming grief and the morbid reality of man's fate. The first few lines of the poem, addressed to the dead infant, set the stage:

Because of you, we, above the ground, are in the same state as you, within it
that which emaciates [us] is like that which consumes you
[It is] as if you took a look at my condition and feared [experiencing] it
if you lived, and so chose death over bereavement
You left the cheeks of the beautiful women with
tears that dissolve the beauty in their big eyes.

(W., 408)

From the very beginning of the poem, al-Mutanabbi undermines the distinction between life and death. Bereavement is a kind of death, he tells us, and those alive after the death of the infant are as good as dead – indeed worse off than the dead. Emaciated – like the obsessed lover of Arabic love poetry – the mourner is worn down, as is the decaying body of the dead child. The economically expressed second line brings together many of the main ideas of the poem. As if to deny the infant's – and every man's – powerlessness over death, the line suggests that the deceased chose death over the potential misery of mourning a loved one. This attribution of imaginary power to the child is shown up for what it is – illusion – via the initial words of the verse: "[It is] as if." In this way, cruel reality is ironically affirmed with more force than a direct statement could have provided.

The first two words of the poem (*bina minka*) are significant, because they echo the sound of the first two words of the famous pre-Islamic ode by Imru'l-Qays, in which he calls upon his two companions to stop and weep with him (*qifa nabki*) over the remains of his beloved's abandoned campsite. It is not just that the two poems are in the same meter and necessarily share the same initial metrical foot; it is that the metrical feet are divided into words of exactly the same musical measure. They thus serve, on a subliminal level, to summon up, in the context of an elegy, the quintessential example of an amatory prelude contained in one of the most famous and esteemed ancient Arabic odes. This is confirmed in the third line, where the effect the child's death had on the female mourners is described. Here, the traditional amatory prelude has been called up, only to be subverted. The effect of this death is to negate the traditional motif: the beautiful women, cried over in the amatory prelude, are replaced by female mourners who cry tears of blood that dissolve their beauty. The decay of death rots not only the infant and his mourner, but also the conventional heroic stance of the lover-poet, eroded like the traces of the beloved's abode lingered over in earlier odes. Throughout the poem, the inevitability of death is emphasized by comparing the earth to a womb – one that will not let go of its contents, or one that forcibly weans the child only to devour him before he was old enough to eat. This reminder that the elegized is a small baby acts as a leitmotif throughout the poem, exaggerating the pathos when it might seem to abate, and serves to emphasize that death, like birth, is universal, the fate of us all.

In this poetic landscape, where the overwhelming message is of powerlessness, the main message of consolation that al-Mutanabbi offers Sayf al-Dawlah is more than a little ironic. The poet manages to paint Sayf al-Dawlah as a hero in this tragic context first by emphasizing the distinction between his private world, currently defined by overwhelming sadness and grief, and his public domain and role as ruler and warrior. He urges endurance on the prince, reminding him that everyone else models their behavior on his. His greatness, the poem affirms, and that of his kin are a distraction from sadness, which they are too busy accomplishing noble deeds to indulge. This distinction between the private and public domains of Sayf al-Dawlah, with their differing demands, peaks in line 12 with its direct address to the patron, where a play on part of the name of the dead infant brings the idea to a point.

> [You] abide in every abode of combat
> as if, with all swords, you are among kin.
>
> (W., 410)

The word used for "combat" in this line is *hayja'*, which is part of the name of Sayf al-Dawlah's son, named Abu'l-Hayja' after his grandfather. "Abu'l-Hayja' " is an agnomen that literally means "the father [in the sense of possessor or dispenser] of war." Powerless to protect his private abode, his household and family – and indeed the emotionally charged abode of the amatory prelude – Sayf al-Dawlah is master over the abodes of the public sphere of battle. Praising Sayf al-Dawlah requires that the abodes of personal attachment be supplanted by the abodes of war, and the contrast between the two is emphasized by the use of the word *hayja'*. From this perspective, Sayf al-Dawlah is a hero, devoted to greater things than the limited universe of family, and the death that pains him now is the same death that he takes charge of and heroically dispenses on the battlefield. Al-Mutanabbi spells out this point of view in line 29 of the poem:

> Is the beloved boy anything but a diversion
> and intimacy with a beautiful woman aught but pain to the husband?
>
> (W., 413)

This might have been a convincing strategy for consoling Sayf al-Dawlah and re-constituting his sense of mastery and strength after the enormous blow of losing his child, were it not for the philosophical backdrop that the poet gave this poem. The lament for Abu'l-Hayja' and the panegyric of Sayf al-Dawlah are punctuated throughout by a series of pessimistic verses about the nature of fate and the futility of life, given the inevitability of pain and death. The final verse of the poem, which effectively vitiates the portrait of worldly heroism just painted for Sayf al-Dawlah, is the culmination of this attitude.

> Fate does not merit that one hope for life
> or yearn for progeny in it.
>
> (W., 414)

Sayf al-Dawlah is a hero because he takes matters into his own hands, despite the inevitability of death and suffering, but he can do nothing to change the grim rules of the game. Ultimately, he has no control.

If anyone comes out a hero in this poem, it is the poet, who sets himself up as the voice of wisdom and guidance to the distraught and overcome Sayf al-Dawlah. With the plural first-person pronoun of the first line, the poetic voice assumes inclusion in the inner circle of the bereaved family, a member of whom would most customarily be expected to compose an elegy on the deceased child. He assumes a level of intimacy sufficient to allow not only the almost macabre dwelling on the decaying corpse of the infant, but also the harsh counsel about the vainness of conjugal intimacy and family life and the superior value of Sayf al-Dawlah's princely role. He goes so far in his bold admonitions that he must justify them in verse 30 – "I have tasted the sweetness of children in youth, / so do not think I have said what I've said in ignorance," and in the following line goes on to place himself and his wisdom a notch above fate itself – "Time is not capable of all I know of it / and the days cannot write what I could dictate." He is claiming, to borrow Julia Bray's translation of the first hemistich of this line, that "I know more of Time than Time itself" (Ashtiany [now Bray], 1997, 372). Fate, the ultimate arbiter of the glory and mastery claimed by the hero Sayf al-Dawlah, is outdone by the poet dispensing absolute knowledge and wisdom to his patron. We saw at the beginning of the poem how the death of the infant resulted in the inversion of the traditional amatory prelude of the Arabic ode; here we see that the praise used to resuscitate the grieving father is itself hollowed out. Other than the inevitability of death and suffering and the fate that brings them, the only absolute left standing by the end of the piece is the all-wise voice of the poet. The poet thus trumps the patron, represented as dependent on the poet for a true understanding of life and death. Verses such as this one, if taken as anything more than extravagant hyperbole, argue forcefully for the notion that al-Mutanabbi did indeed suffer from delusions of grandeur and imagined himself the possessor of some special understanding or knowledge, usually thought of, in an Islamic context, to be the prerogative only of prophets.

THE POET–PATRON RELATIONSHIP

What are the implications of this temerity for the relationship between Sayf al-Dawlah and al-Mutanabbi? In general terms, the brief of the professional poet was to enhance the reputation of his patron through grand poems of eulogy. While panegyric was his primary vehicle, elegy often functioned similarly: hence the old bromide describing elegy as "panegyric in the past tense." Not only did these praise poems customarily laud the patron for the long-honored Arab virtues of valor and generosity, but they also inculcated whatever ideology of the patron's rule he wanted purveyed. For the early 'Abbasid caliphs, this involved portraying the ruler as the divinely guided leader of the Muslim community, whose caliphate entailed the enactment of traditional Arab social values. Poetry commissioned by these caliphs often presented not only a portrait of the leader of the community, but also a definition of the community itself, and the poet became both publicist and political propagandist. As the prestige of a given poet increased, so did his worth to potential patrons, for he became, to the rich and famous, a potent status symbol and mark of their exalted position.

In return for the invaluable press he provided, the poet was well paid – in money, clothing, horses, land, and status. During his days in Aleppo, al-Mutanabbi amassed a fortune, which he guarded jealously. He owned land, had an elaborate entourage, and a household with numerous slaves and servants. This was no small accomplishment for someone who hailed from a modest background. However, for al-Mutanabbi, it was not all about wealth. Numerous poems, including the elegy on Sayf al-Dawlah's infant son, and his youthful revolutionary activities, suggest that his self-image and his ambitions sometimes extended beyond the realms of wealth and even of poetry. In this elegy it is clear that al-Mutanabbi is amplifying the role granted to the poet in a conventional poet–patron relationship. Al-Mutanabbi is not content just to derive riches and renown from his heroic portrayal of his patron; rather, he forces his subject to share the role of hero with him. If Sayf al-Dawlah is the savior of Islam, who boldly beats back the aggressions of the Byzantine Christians and the Bedouin Arab tribes, al-Mutanabbi is his counselor and wise guide. If Sayf al-Dawlah defies death and punishes his enemies in battle, it is the poet who interprets these acts and grasps their true significance in the grander scheme of things. If Sayf al-Dawlah is loyal, affectionate, and generous, it is al-Mutanabbi who comprehends the fleeting nature of personal attachment and appreciates the ultimately tragic nature of man's destiny. Thus virtually every eulogy of Sayf al-Dawlah is to some extent also a eulogy of the poet.

Every great poet who possessed an eager and attentive public wielded real power in pre-modern Arab society. A poet could, with the stroke of his pen or the twist of his tongue, seriously damage the reputation and prestige of his subject with a piece of derogatory satire or invective, and poets were often not above explicitly reminding their patrons of the social and political impact of their poetry. Al-Mutanabbi's concept of his own power and importance, however, went beyond an appreciation of the influence of his poetry, just as his bragging exceeded the bounds of the culturally accepted custom of boasting. From his poetry, it seems he envisioned himself as a seer, entitled, by virtue of his wisdom, to power and status.

Sayf al-Dawlah, in turn, seems to have had extraordinary patience with al-Mutanabbi's pride and indulged his self-importance in numerous ways. The fact that al-Mutanabbi, unlike other poets, was not required to kiss the ground before his patron and was permitted to recite his poems before the prince while seated, rather than standing in respect, is indicative of the latitude Sayf al-Dawlah regularly granted his favorite panegyrist. Both patron and poet understood that, to a certain extent, the public perception of the patron's greatness was determined by the greatness of the poet who panegyrized him. Sayf al-Dawlah knew that he had the best in al-Mutanabbi, and al-Mutanabbi took maximum advantage of it.

DEMANDS ON THE POET

Despite the favored position that al-Mutanabbi enjoyed with Sayf al-Dawlah, there were serious and continuous demands on him – some more appealing than others. Once an inept horseman, who had bravado rather than real skill, al-Mutanabbi became the regular companion of Sayf al-Dawlah in battle, riding alongside his patron and fighting next to him, even in situations where professional soldiers were fleeing the field. His primary function on these occasions was to record the details of the battles and describe them in celebratory panegyrics. Whether Sayf al-Dawlah was victorious or not mattered little, and the demand for eulogistic renditions sometimes led to ridiculous exaggerations of meager, even non-existent, triumphs. On one occasion, al-Mutanabbi was required to produce an ode about a military campaign he had not participated in. More absurd still, Sayf al-Dawlah rejected the poet's first submission because it was lacking in details, and al-Mutanabbi had to compose a second poem on the battle that he had not witnessed.

Military campaigns were not the only occasions for al-Mutanabbi's odes. He was also called on to produce odes on ceremonial occasions, such as visits by Byzantine emissaries to the court at Aleppo. In the several odes composed on these occasions, the poet strove to give his patron the upper hand in the ensuing negotiations by exaggerating his power and status and diminishing that of the Christian visitors.

The poet was often called upon to produce shorter pieces on the spur of the moment. This was not al-Mutanabbi's natural inclination; he much preferred to compose his poems in private and to have the opportunity to edit and revise before reciting them in public. Still, when called on, he quickly composed a poem to undo the jinx of a tent falling down in the Muslim camp shortly before a battle, and another to rally the flagging spirits of the troops in the middle of a battle when the outcome was uncertain. He produced poems on the breaking of the Ramadan fast and on Sayf al-Dawlah's recovery from illness.

Sayf al-Dawlah exacted a steady stream of compositions from the poets he supported, and during his nine years at the Aleppan court al-Mutanabbi composed some forty odes and thirty-one shorter "occasional" poems. Sayf al-Dawlah also expected the poets to participate actively in the diverse intellectual debates and discussions that took place in the court assemblies, and al-Mutanabbi was known to stay up all night to prepare for some of these gatherings. During his recitations of poetry to Sayf al-Dawlah, he had to endure the critical commentary of the prince, who did not hesitate to find fault with individual verses and suggest how they might be improved. While this was common practice among patrons of poetry, it cannot have been easy for the exceedingly proud al-Mutanabbi.

EPIC OCCASIONS

One of al-Mutanabbi's most famous odes ("Resolutions occur according to the measure of the people of resolve ...") was composed to celebrate Sayf al-Dawlah's recapture of the fortress town of Hadath from the Byzantines. Sayf al-Dawlah seized this important frontier town in October, 954, but the Byzantines, with a huge multi-racial army, immediately re-attacked and stalled his efforts to rebuild it. Heavy fighting led to victory when Sayf al-Dawlah managed to capture several members of the Byzantine leader's family. Al-Mutanabbi recited this ode in November, after the rebuilding had been successfully completed. The forty-six-line poem is remarkably reminiscent of the one composed by al-Mutanabbi's predecessor, Abu Tammam, on the occasion of the capture of Amorium by the 'Abbasid caliph, al-Mu'tasim. Like Abu Tammam's, this ode commences with two gnomic verses rather than a traditional amatory introduction:

> Resolutions occur according to the measure of the people of resolve
> and according to the measure of noble people come noble deeds.
> In the eyes of the small, their small deeds are great
> and small in the eyes of the great are great deeds.
>
> (W., 548)

The structural and rhetorical features of these two verses – the symmetry of the chiasmus and the balanced antithesis of the contrasting terms – facilitate the expression of a universal truth, which the poet illustrates in succeeding verses by a description of Sayf al-Dawlah's spectacular military victory. Fate is not mentioned at this point in the poem, and credit for excellence is assigned to the innate nobility of those who manifest it. Sayf al-Dawlah is portrayed as having dominion over fate, but, more importantly, he is described in epic terms as acting in the name of Islam, after the fashion of Abu Tammam's caliph, to "restore [the city] to the [true] religion" through the direct intercession of God. This is what separates this ode from any of the numerous hyperbolic encomiums that al-Mutanabbi produced for his patron. The poet spells out this view in verses such as:

> And you are not a king bringing defeat to his peer,
> but rather monotheism vanquishing polytheism
>
> And why would the Most Merciful not forever protect your two edges,
> when through you He is forever splitting the skulls of the enemy?
>
> (W., 556)

The counterpoint to al-Mutanabbi's praise of Sayf al-Dawlah is a series of verses in which the Byzantine domesticus and his army are lampooned. The approach of the motley army of many nationalities, so laden with armor that their horses looked as if they had no feet, is painted as a scene of ludicrous turmoil. It is this jumble of men, armor, and languages that will become orderly and unified as a result of Sayf al-Dawlah's military success. In contrast to Sayf al-Dawlah's valor, the domesticus is an obvious coward ("Does that domesticus advance [upon you] every day,/his neck blaming his face for advancing?" [W., 554]), thanking his companions as he flees for keeping the Muslim swords busy with their skulls and not his own.

There are a number of noteworthy features in the composition of this carefully crafted poem. Following the example of al-Buhturi and Abu Tammam, al-Mutanabbi, perhaps even more effectively, uses onomatapoeia to convey the sounds and sights of the intense battle scene. The manipulation of the music of the diction, one of the outstanding characteristics of al-Mutanabbi's art, is particularly prominent. Words that are semantically related or contribute to the same theme are linked together through rhyming words, connected by assonance and/or derivation from the same roots (paronomasia).

Not only does this feature render the poem easy to remember, it also contributes to a strikingly unified structure. As Latham has pointed out, the poem also possesses a marked simplicity of diction and grammar, so that "it is almost as if the poet is proclaiming his intention of bringing the achievement of Sayf before a much wider audience of the faithful than would otherwise have been possible" (Latham, 1979, 12). In my opinion, this is one of the relatively unexplored reasons for al-Mutanabbi's immense popularity with successive generations of Arab consumers. Al-Mutanabbi was not trying to be Abu'l-'Atahiya (748–826 CE), an 'Abbasid poet who specifically tried to create for himself a niche in the poetic market as one who composed for the man in the street. Al-Mutanabbi remained firmly within the grand tradition, but opened the door to that elite style and made it accessible to a broader audience.

The Hadath ode is propaganda poetry, intended to promote the image of Sayf al-Dawlah as the savior of Islam rather than a petty ruler with dominion over a limited region and populace. The pre-Islamic Arab belief in fate as the arbiter of life and death is supplanted by an Islamic religio-political ideology that Sayf al-Dawlah is credited with upholding as bravely and dedicatedly as the earlier 'Abbasid caliph, al-Mu'tasim, celebrated in Abu Tammam's ode on the capture of Amorium. It is not just Sayf al-Dawlah's essential Arabness – astutely evoked by features such as the description of his slaughter of enemies in battle, directly derived from the quintessentially Arab sport of falconry (Latham, 1979, 18) – that is lauded, but also his role as Arab champion of the Islamic community. Appropriately, this ode contains far less self-aggrandizing than is common in al-Mutanabbi's poetry. The one mildly boastful moment, an expression of an idealized poet–patron relationship, occurs in verse 41: "The praise for the pearls that I articulate is yours/you are its giver, and I its arranger" (W., 555), but even this retains its focus on the eulogizing of the patron. The poem is thus a well-modulated encomium that compellingly establishes Sayf al-Dawlah as equal to the caliph, and al-Mutanabbi as equal to the great epic poets of the 'Abbasid era.

TROUBLE IN PARADISE

Al-Mutanabbi's privileged position in the court at Aleppo inevitably roused the ire and jealousy of a number of his poet and scholar colleagues. He was not the only panegyrist in Sayf al-Dawlah's entourage, and there was great competition for the admiration, and especially the rewards, dispensed by the prince. Al-Mutanabbi was seen by many to be hogging the show, and his natural arrogance added fuel to the conspiratorial fire. For example, early in 952, in one of the first signs of trouble between al-Mutanabbi and his enemies, he declared provocatively in the course of a poem to his patron: "My two friends, I do not see other than one poet, / so how is it that from them comes the claim [to be poets] and from me the poems?" (W., 463)

We will never know for sure, but it seems likely that things would have turned out differently for al-Mutanabbi if his major adversary at court had been anyone other than Sayf al-Dawlah's cousin, Abu Firas al-Hamdani (932–968 CE), himself a poet of the first rank. Abu Firas had his cousin's ear and seized every available opportunity to argue the case against al-Mutanabbi on behalf of the growing cohort of rivals. On one occasion he said to his cousin: "This big-mouth takes too much liberty with you. Every year you give him thousands of dinars for three odes, when you could distribute two hundred dinars among twenty poets who would produce poetry better than his" (*al-Subh al-munabbi*, 87–88). Sayf al-Dawlah is said to have taken his cousin's advice to heart and acted on it while al-Mutanabbi was away. On his return, the poet attempted to smooth things over with his patron with a six-line apology poem, which ends with an appeal for forgiveness, based on one of the sayings of the prophet Muhammad: "He who repents a sin is like one who is sinless." The verse reads: "Even if mine were the worst of offenses / he who repents wipes out the sin completely" (W., 487). However, al-Mutanabbi's presumptuous behavior, including his occasional refusal to compose any new poetry, had taken its toll on his relationship with his patron, and this brief poem failed to produce the desired effect. A much grander ode consisting of thirty-seven lines of apology, reprimand, praise, and boasting followed. This poem ("Alas, for the burning of my heart ...") was recited in the presence of Abu Firas and his fellow agitators, who kept up a steady chorus of accusations and heckling throughout.

In this ode, al-Mutanabbi presents himself as a tormented lover, aggrieved by the mistreatment of Sayf al-Dawlah. His goal is to remind his patron of his worth as a poet and establish his superiority over Abu Firas in composition and affection. He boldly declares that Sayf al-Dawlah has been unjust and appeals to him to be discriminating.

> Alas, for the burning of my heart on account of one whose heart is cold
> and because of whom my body and soul are sick
> Why should I hide a love that has wasted my flesh,
> when all the nations claim their love for Sayf al-Dawlah?
> And if we are joined in love of his shining brow,
> then may our shares be divided up in proportion to our love
>
> Oh, you most just of people, except in your treatment of me,
> the feud is over you and you are both adversary and judge
> May God guard your faithful eyes
> from supposing fat in one whose fat is [mere] bloating
> For what use does a man have for his eyes
> if lights and darknesses are all the same to him?
>
> (W., 481–483)

The poet then boasts extravagantly of his poetic powers, but is not content to leave it at that. He boldly praises himself, as we have seen him do before, in language normally befitting praise of the patron.

> I am the one whose writing even the blind see
> and the one whose poems have brought hearing to the deaf
> I sleep soundly unconcerned with fugitive verses
> while men keep vigil for them and struggle to extract them
>
> The horses and the night and the barren desert know me,
> so too, war and combat and paper and pen.
>
> (W., 483–484)

Abu Firas, who punctuated the recitation of numerous verses with accusations of plagiarism, did not fail to react against the poet's usurpation of the patron's role as hero. Outraged, he exclaimed: "What have you left to the prince if you attribute bravery, eloquence, leadership, and generosity to yourself? You praise yourself with [verses] you've stolen from others and take the prince's rewards" (*al-Subh al-munabbi*, 90). As some renditions have it, Sayf al-Dawlah was so vexed by the accumulation of charges against al-Mutanabbi that he threw an ink bottle at him. To this insult, al-Mutanabbi replied with the following disarming, if hackneyed, verse: "If what our envier said delighted you/a wound that pleases you causes no pain" (W., 484). Despite Abu Firas' citation of two precedents, Sayf al-Dawlah appreciated the verse, kissed the poet's head, and gave him two thousand dinars (*al-Subh al-munabbi*, 91).

In this poem, which is a mixture of expressions of hurt and bold reproach, al-Mutanabbi suggests that he might leave Sayf al-Dawlah's court, though he would regret it, and puts the responsibility for his decision squarely in the hands of the patron. A curious group of verses early in the poem, ostensibly meant to laud Sayf al-Dawlah's valor in battle, must have given the prince serious pause. Rather than painting the familiar scene of triumphant military prowess and bravery, the poet focuses on the case where the enemy flees the battlefield, obviating the need for Sayf al-Dawlah to exercise his military might. While on the one hand, he is reminding Sayf al-Dawlah that he has been with him through thick and thin, he is primarily reminding him that the interpretation of what is thick and what is thin ultimately lies in the hands of this uniquely gifted poet:

> I have visited him when the Indian swords were sheathed,
> and I have seen him when the swords were full of blood
>
> The fleeing of the enemy you sought was a victory:
> as it contains regret, so it holds blessings
>
> It is your job to defeat them in every encounter,
> but it is no disgrace to you if they are put to flight.
>
> (W., 481–482)

There is one verb in the last verse above that tells the whole story of the rhetorical power al-Mutanabbi is reminding the prince he possesses. "Are put to flight" is an inadequate translation of what is actually, in Arabic, a reflexive verb. In Arabic, this verb form (Form VII) suggests that the action referred to occurred without the agency of any actor. It is not just that the agent is not mentioned, but rather as if there were none at all. The message, and its implicit threat, cannot have escaped Sayf al-Dawlah: al-Mutanabbi is reminding him of the rhetorical – and, ultimately, political – power he possesses. It is he, "whose poems have brought hearing to the deaf," who will tell the tale of Sayf al-Dawlah's feats in the fashion that he sees fit. He spins things in whatever way he wishes.

This poem is not all bluster or jockeying for power. A number of verses reveal al-Mutanabbi's sincere disappointment, along with a true sense of abandonment. He says, for example, in verse 34: "The worst of lands is a place where there is no friend / and the worst thing a man can acquire is that which dishonors him" (W., 486), and concludes the poem with: "This is a reproach to you, except that it is a show of affection / inlaid with pearls, except they are words" (W., 486).

Sayf al-Dawlah's positive reception of this ode did little to alter the behavior of al-Mutanabbi's enemies. Two failed assassination attempts followed, the second with the support of Abu'l-'Asha'ir, Sayf al-Dawlah's cousin and al-Mutanabbi's former patron in Antioch. As a result, the poet went into hiding and stayed there until Sayf al-Dawlah had assured him of his support and guaranteed his safety. The reconciliation was sealed by a grand ceremony in which al-Mutanabbi officially returned to court and Sayf al-Dawlah's inner circle.

AL-MUTANABBI BITES BACK

Never one to quit while he was ahead, al-Mutanabbi persisted in his taunting of Abu Firas and the other court poets aligned against him. Not only did the poet compose mocking epigrams in direct response to his detractors, but also included sections dedicated to boasting and explicit derision of his enemies in poems for diverse occasions. In a poem composed in 953, on the occasion of the visit to the Hamdanid court of Byzantine emissaries who had come to negotiate the release of prisoners captured by Sayf al-Dawlah, al-Mutanabbi included:

> Through Sayf al-Dawlah, the light, I have attained such a rank
> that I illuminate through it everything that is between west and east
> When he wants to trifle with a fool [among the poets]
> he shows him the trail of my dust and tells him to catch up with me
> Causing grief to my enviers is not something I intended
> but whosoever takes on the sea will surely drown
> The prince uses his intelligence to test people
> and looks the other way, despite knowing which ones are prattlers
> Turning the eyes away is of no use
> when the heart does not [also] turn away.
>
> (W., 503–504)

Similarly, in a poem composed in April 954, on the Feast of the Sacrifice, sixty days after the end of the Ramadan fast, he exclaims: "Reward me whenever [any] poetry is recited to you for/the panegyrists bring you [nothing but] my poetry repeated" (W., 535).

ALL GOOD THINGS ...

The intention to repair the relationship between poet and patron seems to have been sincere on both sides. Al-Mutanabbi clearly felt secure in his position at court. We saw, in the verse "Turning the eyes away ...," that he felt confident enough to include an explicit demand that Sayf al-Dawlah's change in attitude be a true rejection of his detractors and not merely a superficial shunning of them. Al-Mutanabbi composed some of his most celebrated poetry, including the Hadath poem, after his re-entry into the Hamdanid's graces in early 953. None the less, the apparent lack of composition by al-Mutanabbi for periods as long as six months suggests that something was amiss. Even after al-Mutanabbi had given up responding to Abu Firas and his other critics in his poetry, he still had to deal with them in Sayf al-Dawlah's assemblies and private gatherings. It was on one such occasion that al-Mutanabbi's pride and bad manners got the best of him.

As the story goes, one of the many scholarly debates that took place at court degenerated into a competition between al-Mutanabbi and the grammarian, Ibn Khalawayh. Although al-Mutanabbi was clearly winning the battle, he saw fit to insult Ibn Khalawayh with the comment: "You'd better keep still. You're a Persian from Khuzistan. What do you have to do with the Arabic language?" (*al-Subh al-munabbi*, 87). Furious, Ibn Khalawayh hit the poet in the face with a key: in some accounts of this incident, al-Mutanabbi's comment occurred as a reaction to Ibn Khalawayh's pulling out his key and threatening the poet. Either way, the end result was the same and al-Mutanabbi ended up with blood all over his face. When Sayf al-Dawlah failed to intervene or comment, it was clear that al-Mutanabbi's days at the Hamdanid court had come to an end.

Shortly after this incident, the poet requested, and received, Sayf al-Dawlah's permission to visit an estate he owned in Syria. This was merely a pretext to leave Aleppo accompanied by his entire household and carrying with him all the treasures he had acquired during his stay there.

It was mid-957 and al-Mutanabbi was forty-two years old. Once again, he was without a patron and setting out to find a new base of support in a new political environment. The difference was that by now he had become a well-known and keenly sought-after poet of some distinction.

4

PARADISE LOST

FROM ALEPPO TO EGYPT

Al-Mutanabbi headed for Damascus, then under the control of the Ikhshidid dynasty, which had split the territory of Syria with its rivals, the Hamdanids. In Damascus, al-Mutanabbi was received by the governor, Ibn Malik, whose ambition to be panegyrized by the now famous poet met with a cool reception.

When the Ikhshidid regent of Egypt, Abu'l-Misk Kafur, wrote to Ibn Malik to send al-Mutanabbi to the Egyptian capital of Fustat, the rebuffed governor was only too glad to send a refusal to Kafur in al-Mutanabbi's name, potentially stirring up trouble for the poet. Al-Mutanabbi sought refuge with his old friend, al-Hasan, governor of Ramlah, where he probably would have stayed had Kafur not demanded the poet come to Egypt. Even after his arrival at Fustat in August of 957, to a grand reception at Kafur's opulent court, al-Mutanabbi, who may have had his eye on the court of one of the Ikhshidid viziers, resisted the regent's overtures. Only with the promise of a governorship, perhaps of Sidon, was Kafur able to win over the poet, and in September of that year al-Mutanabbi recited his first poem as official panegyrist to Kafur.

In this first panegyric to Kafur ("It is sickness enough ..."), it was important, as Suzanne Stetkevych has pointed out (*Legitimacy*, 222), that al-Mutanabbi publicly declare his allegiance to his new patron. It is therefore not surprising to find, in its prelude, a disavowal of his former maecenas, Sayf al-Dawlah. This is followed by generous praise of the Ikhshidid regent, Kafur, in which the poet went so far as to suggest that Sayf al-Dawlah reigned only at the indulgence of Kafur, who had in fact been successful in both battle and negotiation against the Hamdanids.

Despite its apparent allegiance to the protocol of panegyric, this poem has some exceptional features. Al-Mutanabbi's arch-rival, Abu 'Ali Muhammad ibn al-Hasan al-Hatimi, to whom we will return, criticized the poet for opening this ode in a manner more suitable to elegies. His objection focused on the idea that a bad omen could be drawn from the first line of the poem, with its mention of death and illness. (*al-Risalah al-mudihah*, 67; *al-Subh al-munabbi*, 300) While there is intuitive wisdom in this comment, it misses the originality of the poem. Two features coalesce to make this an unusual and noteworthy panegyric: the very emotional tenor of the poet's references to his former friend, Sayf al-Dawlah, and the equivocal nature of much of his praise for his new patron, Kafur.

The forlorn addressee of the opening verses is represented as being totally alone in the world. Without human attachment, either feigned or sincere, he wishes for death. Addressing his heart, which is his innermost being and essential nature, the poet chides it for feeling the loss of its former love — here, clearly, the lost friend and protector, Sayf al-Dawlah. Implementing the power belonging to any professional poet in his situation, al-Mutanabbi rhetorically vitiates the praise he had formerly heaped on Sayf al-Dawlah:

> If generosity is not granted secure from molestation
> then praise is not earned, and wealth does not endure
> The individual has moral values that define the man:
> Was it generosity he showed or feigned liberality?
>
> (W., 624)

But the tone of hurt and personal loss betrays an attachment and an emotional engagement that goes beyond the sting of a severed professional relationship.

> Decrease your longing, my heart: Oh, how much
> sincere affection I see you showing one who does not requite it

I was created so amiable that if I journeyed back to youth,
I would leave old age with a pained heart, in tears.

(W., 624)

This lament for the lost love, here Sayf al-Dawlah, is followed by a contrasting picture of al-Mutanabbi's new patron. Kafur is "a sea" of generosity (v. 13), who makes the poet forget "rivulets," such as Sayf al-Dawlah. (v. 20) He is one who performs only "virgin" acts of nobility (v. 24) and in whom "the Most Merciful has combined ... all good qualities" (v. 29).

But interspersed among verses of manifest praise of Kafur are some that are more equivocal. As custom demanded, the poet praises Kafur for his military prowess and his bravery in war, yet some of the verses relating to this topic can be read as dismissive of Kafur's actual agency on the field of battle. It is customary to describe the accoutrements and companions of the warrior – his spear, sword, horses, and army – as possessing the attributes for which the patron is being praised. In this poem, however, the people and objects associated with Kafur are often presented as being the real holders and executors of power. For example, al-Mutanabbi praises Kafur for leading to battle squadrons that cross desert wastelands to trample diverse tribes (v. 40), and specifies: "You have raided the homes of kings with them, and their hooves/ have flattened their skulls and their abodes" (v. 41) (W., 628). There is much that is laudatory here: Kafur's might is measured by the extensive and fierce army he commands and by the grandeur of those he defeats. But it is "*their* hands" that did the trampling of the enemy kings, not Kafur's. Instead of focusing on how the army acquires its might from their leader, Kafur, the poet focuses on how Kafur is victorious thanks to his army. In line 38, Kafur's sword is described as so fierce that it refuses to spare even those its owner exempts. While this line applauds Kafur's ferocity and the swiftness of his sword, it also portrays the patron as being not completely in control and possessing the blameworthy characteristic of *jahl*, or rashness, rather than the desired *hilm*, or prudence, of the true hero. A comparison with al-Mutanabbi's hyperbolic praise of the warrior Sayf al-Dawlah makes it clear that the poet is making a deliberate rhetorical choice in the measured quality of his praise for Kafur. Consider, in contrast, these verses recited for Sayf al-Dawlah as he was leaving Byzantine territory after battle:

> And one well-tempered sword that gave orders to death,
> which obeyed as if obeying the All-Merciful
>
> Swords side with those whose hearts are
> like their own, when two armies meet.
>
> (v. 41, 44) (W., 599)

In both cases, the swords are personified as a metonymy for their wielder. The contrast exists in the relationship between the two halves of the metonymy, the sword and its bearer. For Sayf al-Dawlah, his temperament retains mastery: it is *his* attitude that dictates the behavior of the swords and it is only through him that they are able to function.

The new poem contains verses of unconditional praise of Kafur – the poet was, after all, a paid panegyrist. But the scattering of more restrained – even subtly ironic – lines in between the blatantly complimentary ones has the effect of flattening the tone so that the praise never reaches the hyperbolic crescendo of the panegyrics to Sayf al-Dawlah. Constrained by the demands of his profession to praise Kafur, al-Mutanabbi found a way to maneuver around the dictates of convention to express his personal reservations.

RELUCTANT PRAISE

In contrast to Sayf al-Dawlah, Kafur wasn't al-Mutanabbi's idea of an ideal master. He was a Nubian slave, sold at the age of ten to Muhammad ibn Tughj al-Ikhshid, the founder of the Ikhshidid dynasty, which ruled over Egypt and southern Syria during the tenth century (935–969 CE). His name, meaning "camphor," to denote intense whiteness, in contrast to the extreme blackness of his skin, was given to him by al-Ikhshid. Having gained his master's trust and respect, Kafur became first the tutor of al-Ikhshid's two sons and eventually, during the reign of the princes, regent, with almost total authority. After the death of the second prince, Kafur declared himself ruler of Egypt. His military prowess was matched by shrewd negotiation and management skills; during his reign, despite severe military, social, and economic challenges, Egypt enjoyed security and economic stability.

An unabashed apologist for Arab racial superiority who mourned the loss of military and political power to non-Arab rulers, al-Mutanabbi now had to sing the praises of a eunuch and former slave rather than a mighty Arab hero of Sayf al-Dawlah's ilk. It makes sense, therefore, that some verses of this first panegyric to Kafur can be read as suggesting that the regent's own sense of greatness was his alone and quite unwarranted. Lines 34 and 35, for example, which praise Kafur's high ambitions, can also be read as accusing him of grandiosity:

> You are not one who attained kingship by wishing
> but rather by battles that turned the forelocks white
> Your enemies see them as incursions into territories
> while you see them as stairs to the heavens

(W., 627)

The closeness of line 33 to the Qur'anic verse, "All that is on it (the earth) perishes, while the face of your Lord remains" (55:26–27), noted by Sperl and Shackle (*Qasida Poetry in Islamic Asia and Africa*, vol. 2, 421, n. 8), has a nearly blasphemous tone to it:

> And you despise the world as one who has tested it,
> seeing all that is in it – save yourself – as ephemeral.

(W., 627)

Al-Mutanabbi's emphasis on the hard-won nature of Kafur's status – on the face of it, admiration of his ambition, tenacity, and efficiency – can also be interpreted as an oblique reference to his patron's lowly origins. The common conceit of praising the individual drive and merit of a patron with an impressive lineage, here rings hollow, and emphasizes that Kafur in fact had no lineal laurels to rest on. This double-edged reference to Kafur's rise to power culminates in the very laden line 45, when the poet says: "[It is] the utmost degree, which the master's lord caused him to reach/as did the soul he has, which would not be satisfied with anything but reaching the limit" (W., 629). Most commentators take the phrase "his lord" to refer to God, but it could also refer to Kafur's temporal master, the Ikhshid, who was responsible for his ascendance. Such an interpretation is especially invited by the equivocal term, *al-ustadh* (the master), in the same line. This is both an honorific, denoting one who is accomplished and possesses esteem and authority ("master" or "chief") and a synonym for "eunuch." Even as the poet apparently praises Kafur's ambition and success, he simultaneously evokes his former status as slave and suggests that were it not for "his lord – and master," he would not have wound up a "master" himself.

This two-pronged praise is in the same vein as the poet's constant reference in his eulogistic metaphors to his patron's skin color, despite the fact that Kafur was known to dislike mention of it. Fustat became the scene of al-Mutanabbi's greatest production of satire and invective. More interesting than the straightforward insult poems were those in which the poet sustained the veneer of panegyric, while using irony to create an underlayer of mockery. Later on, in Baghdad, al-Mutanabbi edited his *diwan*, so it is impossible for us to know whether he really got away with saying all he is recorded as having said in his poems to Kafur or whether he later edited them to make his mockery bolder than circumstances originally allowed.

Kafur would have been a challenge for any professional panegyrist, as Blachère points out. Not only was he without the exalted lineage a poet would normally extol, but he also lacked even a modicum of the physical beauty that could often serve as the stuff of panegyric. The paucity of dramatic military encounters during al-Mutanabbi's years in Egypt also meant that this customary fodder for heroic praise poetry was missing (*Poète arabe*, 198–199). There is little doubt that, for al-Mutanabbi, whose grandiosity fed to a large extent on the heroic stature of his subject, praising Kafur was a demeaning activity. If al-Mutanabbi's pride and prejudices inclined him to be less than enthusiastic in his praise of Kafur, his hunger for the promised governorship kept him in line. Unlike his custom at Aleppo, in Egypt al-Mutanabbi stood to recite poetry. Decked out in boots and girded with waist-belt and sword, al-Mutanabbi presented himself in pathetic burlesque, aiming at impressing the regent with his battle-readiness and seriousness of purpose (*al-Subh al-munabbi*, 112). In the Egyptian court, his poetry alternated between fawning praise of Kafur and increasingly impatient demands for the pledged position of authority. For the next few years, Kafur and al-Mutanabbi played cat and mouse, with the poet reminding his patron of his promise and the patron attempting to distract him from his demands with gifts and generous payment. The poet was sumptuously rewarded for his poetic labors, and lived an even more luxurious life than he had in Aleppo.

The Ikhshidids were avid supporters of scholarship and the arts; not only the regent, but many of his viziers and officials presided over vibrant courts where poets, philologists, and diverse intellectuals thrived. By the time al-Mutanabbi transferred to Fustat, his reputation was so well established that, in public, even his enemies had to remain respectful. He outshone the Ikhshidid stable of poets – many of whom were chancellery secretaries – who focused mainly on love and wine poetry, and stood out for his mastery of panegyric. At Fustat, he continued the practice he had established at Aleppo of presiding over a circle of admirers and students, who came from far and near to benefit from the poet's commentary on his poems. Fustat and the poet's seminars became a stopover on the pilgrimage route of Andalusian and North African poets and scholars, who thus conveyed al-Mutanabbi's poetry to the Arab west. From there, it was to shape the work of generations of poets writing in Arabic, extending al-Mutanabbi's prestige as leader of arguably the most influential school of poetry in the history of Arabic verse.

AL-MUTANABBI DEMANDS HIS DUE

In a panegyric recited in 958, some seven months after al-Mutanabbi's arrival in Fustat, on the occasion of receiving a black colt as a gift from Kafur, al-Mutanabbi presses his patron for the promised political appointment. He hints that he would be able to patch things up with his former patron, Sayf al-Dawlah, who, he now avers, is "not blameworthy" (W., 649), and urges Kafur to fulfill his promise.

> If I knew how long my life would be, I would divide it up
> and gladly commit two thirds of it to waiting for you
> But when time passes, it is gone [forever]
> So bestow on me the share of one ready and eager to reap his spoils
>
> You are like one whose heart is an intercessor
> who spoke to him about me, without me speaking.
>
> (W., 654)

Another piece ("I used to wish that white hair ..."), composed around the end of the same year, conveys just how desperate al-Mutanabbi was for the promised appointment. Many of al-Mutanabbi's compositions contain verses of boasting and self-aggrandizing. The eighteen-line heroic self-portrait that opens this piece stands out not only for its length and the polemical role it plays in the poet's negotiations with Kafur, but also for the tone of personal melancholy that permeates it. Conveyed in the somber voice of an unfulfilled, middle-aged man imploring his patron for what may be his last chance at glory, and juxtaposed with a panegyric to Kafur, this rather long heroic manifesto has a desperate, almost pathetic, ring. As if trying to convince Kafur of his qualifications for political authority, al-Mutanabbi assures him that, despite his age and graying hair, his soul possesses unchanging youth and the ferocity of a tough warrior. Unfettered by attachment to a particular homeland, free of inclination to women and drink, he is a leader among men, with nothing to distract him from his duty. Using the topoi of the "brigand poets" of the highly esteemed pre-Islamic period of Arabic poetry, al-Mutanabbi describes himself as an über-male who is, if anything, over-qualified for the governorship Kafur has dangled before his eyes. A virtual eagle that has no need for a mount, he declares:

> I get thirsty, but show no need of water
> though the sun be streaking gossamer above the swift, hardy camels

> Secrets have a place in me that no drinking companion
> can reach, nor drink arrive at
>
> We have left off all desires for the points of spears
> and we know no recreation except in them
>
> The most noble place in the world is the saddle of a fast horse
> and the best companion ever is a book.
>
> (W., 682–683)

This elaborate boast is followed by praise of Kafur, one verse of which was signaled even by Ibn Jinni, al-Mutanabbi's close protégé and commentator on his poetry, as being so exaggerated that it "almost turns into satire" (al-Barquqi, 1:313).

> He has surpassed the scope of panegyric, as if,
> with the best of praise, he is being censured.
>
> (W., 684)

Unless we read this verse as a satirical commentary on the hyperbole of the entire praise section of this poem, these verses would constitute some of the most unctuous of al-Mutanabbi's panegyrics to Kafur. Stereotypically, Kafur is described as the most voluminous of seas in generosity, a fierce warrior, and the most judicious of rulers. Unlike other sovereigns, he is a true lion, whose inherent superiority would lead men to obey him, if his generosity and the threat of his might did not do so. In an extended apostrophe to his patron, al-Mutanabbi broaches the subject of his unfulfilled ambitions:

> We have a share due from this destiny that it is holding back –
> Fulfillment has been so meager, though reproval has been prolonged
> Fate may act in unaccustomed ways when it comes to you,
> with times becoming populated, when they are desolate.
>
> (W., 685–686)

In this way, he both associates himself with the heroic stature of his patron, and attributes to him the power to manipulate fate as he wishes. Just as he has snatched his due glory from fate (v. 27), so too he is able to tame fate to fulfill al-Mutanabbi's wishes. After first declaring his pleasure at simply being near Kafur, the poet starkly demands:

> Does it benefit me that the curtains between us be raised
> when there is a barrier blocking what I hoped for from you?
>
> (W., 686)

Pulling back, he proceeds:

> I broach the subject rarely in order not to burden you
> and I remain silent so there be no need for you [to bother with] an answer
> My soul has needs that you have the insight [to discern]
> Because of it (i.e., the insight) my silence becomes declaration and speech.
>
> (W., 686)

Suggesting that giving the poet what he wants is in Kafur's own best interest and not vain greed on the poet's part, al-Mutanabbi declares:

> I do not wish anything but to show my critics
> that my view of your love was correct
> and to show a group who, unlike me, went east
> while I went west, that I succeeded while they were disappointed.
>
> (W., 687)

In other poems, al-Mutanabbi was still more direct with lines such as: "If you do not entrust to me a territory or governorship / it is as if your generosity clothes me, and then your indifference strips me" (W., 664).

SAVING FACE AT ALEPPO

As we have seen, attaining the brass ring of political authority with which Kafur had enticed al-Mutanabbi to Fustat was not just a matter of personal pride, but also of saving face before his rivals at his former patron's Hamdanid court. In a poem addressed to Sayf al-Dawlah ("With what can I distract myself …"), composed when al-Mutanabbi learned that his death had been reported to the court at Aleppo, the poet complains bitterly of what he sees as Sayf al-Dawlah's betrayal and abandonment of him and insists on the reliability of Kafur's word:

> The reward to anyone who is close to you is weariness
> and the fortune of anyone who loves you is spite
>
> Separation has left a pathless desert between you and me,
> in which the eye and the ear [both] lie
>
> I do not continue taking wealth that abases me,
> nor can I take pleasure in that which sullies my honor
> After leaving I was sleepless, forlorn over you
> Then I pulled myself together and sleep returned
>
> My colt has worn out his cloths in another's domain
> and his cheek-strap and halter have been replaced at Fustat,
> with the great Abu'l-Misk, in whose generosity
> red Mudar and Yemen are awash
> If some of what he has promised is delayed
> [still] my hopes are neither deferred nor weakened
> He is faithful [to his word] – it is only that I mentioned to him
> my affection and [now] he is putting it to the test.
>
> (W., 669–671)

This poem emphasizes al-Mutanabbi's celebrity, his continued visibility, and the demographics of the audience for his poetry. The poet was still gossiped about in Aleppo and his poems were readily conveyed to his former home and beyond. Thus, for al-Mutanabbi, a great deal was riding on his ability to inveigle Kafur into fulfilling his promise.

KAFUR'S FINAL REFUSAL

By the beginning of 959, the writing was clearly on the walls for al-Mutanabbi. Not only had the supporters he had sent to intercede on his behalf brought back discouraging news, but the poet finally received a forthright refusal when Kafur declared to him: "When you were poor and in a bad way, with no one to support you, you had pretensions to prophethood. If you attained a governorship and acquired a following, who would be able to stand you?" (*al-Subh al-munabbi*, 112)

While some hope remained that al-Mutanabbi could get what he wanted from Kafur, the poet had been able to do his duty as official panegyrist, churning out poems such as a congratulatory piece on the occasion of Kafur's quashing of a plot by supporters of the Ikhshidid prince, Unujur. Now that the hopelessness of his situation was apparent, the poet's natural resistance to praising Kafur was accentuated. When a group of Qarmatian rebels from al-Mutanaabbi's old stomping grounds, led by the Bedouin leader, Shabib al-'Uqayli, raided Damascus, the poem he composed, supposedly to congratulate Kafur, was bold in its unmasked adulation of the rebel chief and the mocking tone of its grudging praise of Kafur. It appears that Shabib did not die in battle with Kafur, but from an accident or natural cause that killed him before the fighting could take place. Some reports have it that the rebel leader suffered a seizure and fell dead on the ground; according to others he had drunk poisoned wine that took effect as he was to go into battle. In any case, his followers were easily dispersed once their leader fell, and Kafur had an easy victory. Unlike poems celebrating Sayf al-Dawlah's serendipitous victories, or even defeats, the poet here assigns the credit for felling Shabib to fate and Kafur's good luck. The lack of agency on the part of the regent, hinted at in his initial poem to Kafur, is spelled out, anchored in the facts of the incident.

The hyperbole of the first line of the poem reaches a level of ludicrousness that even the poet's commentators could not miss: "Your enemy is censured by every tongue/even if the sun and the moon were among your enemies" (W., 672). Shabib merits no shame for his "defeat," the poet makes clear, for death is the fate of every living being (v. 7). In several lines (v. 8–12) of unmitigated praise for the deceased enemy of his patron ("he attained a life desired by his enemy,/and a death that makes every coward long for death"), he makes clear that Shabib was a mighty warrior who died simply because it was his destiny: he could repel the swords of his enemy in battle, but he could not cast off the effect of the stars (v. 10). With the blunt insult to Kafur's valor in line 12 – "He had slain his rivals until you killed him / with the weakest of competitors in the humblest of places" – the regent vocalized his irritation, and claimed credit for having defeated Shabib with "the most severe of competitors in the most exalted of places," that is, the battlefield (al-'Ukbari, 4:244). The poet continues: "Had death travelled the path of arms, he would have repelled / it with the reach of his arm and the scope of his heart" (v. 14) (W., 674), for no great army can reach someone if his death is not ordained (v. 16). His bold challenge to Kafur – "Why do you carry a long-belted sword / when the fates render you without need of it?" (v. 25) – can mean that his teleological station is so exalted that fate does his bidding, but it can also convey, especially in the context of this poem, the notion that Kafur has no real power and is nothing more than the passive beneficiary of fate's kindness. The last two verses offer praise so exaggerated that the intended mockery is easily grasped:

> Wish favor for me, whether you grant it or not,
> for whatever you wish for me will come my way
> If you hated the motion of the revolving globe,
> something would hinder its orbiting.
>
> (W., 675)

This final note, nearly blasphemous in its parodic assigning to Kafur magical power over the celestial bodies, serves as a clear announcement of the true intent of this poem.

ANGRY SATIRE

Al-Mutanabbi had to endure life at Kafur's court for several more years after learning that he had been duped by Kafur's promises. Though he no longer participated in Kafur's private assemblies, he produced poems for public consumption, such as the one just discussed, and he privately vented his anger in a series of unrestrained, and often racist, invectives against the Ikhshidid regent. Like the following, most were devoid of the irony we saw in many of his earlier poems to Kafur, instead emulating the brazenly coarse tone of the Umayyad satirists.

> More stupid than a slave and his woman
> is one who makes a slave his ruler
>
> The slave's nature is concerned with nothing
> but his fetid genitals or his molars
> He does not make good on his promise on the appointed day
> and does not remember what he said yesterday
>
> Do not expect good from a man
> over whose head the slave trader's hand has passed
> If you have doubts about the way he is
> just take a look at his race
>
> Whoever finds a way out of his rank
> cannot [also] get away from his origin.
>
> (W., 654–656)

OUT OF EGYPT

Nothing short of escape from Fustat would satisfy al-Mutanabbi. As early as 960, in a poem written about a fever that laid him up for a long time (W., 679), he spoke longingly about travel and his desire to set out in search of glory. Eager to keep al-Mutanabbi at his court – less now for his panegyrics than for fear of the satires that would be loosed against him if the poet had free rein – Kafur had spies keep him under close watch. When the poet sought permission to go to Ramlah to collect a debt, Kafur would not allow it, no doubt suspecting that his true aim was to seek refuge with his old patron, al-Hasan, governor of Ramlah.

In early January, 962, with the help of friends, al-Mutanabbi managed to slip away amidst the ceremonies in preparation for the yearly pilgrimage to Mecca. The day before his departure, the eve of the Feast of the Sacrifice, he composed a poem of boldly uncensored invective ("Feast day, in what state do you return …"), which he entrusted to associates to deliver to Kafur after he was out of harm's way. Although Kafur burned the poem without having read it, al-Mutanabbi reproduced and disseminated the poem along with the rest of his *oeuvre*. Like most of the poet's invectives from this period, the poem makes scurrilous reference to the slave origin and sexual ambiguity of the eunuch Kafur, and wonders that the likes of him could have attained authority.

> I dwelt among liars, whose guest
> is denied both hospitality and departure
> The generosity of men is from their hands, while their liberality
> is from their tongues – would that neither they nor their generosity existed!
>
> [He is] one of the soft-bellied, bloated ones
> that cannot be counted either a man or a woman
>
> The eunuch has become the lord of runaway slaves there (in Egypt)
> with the freeborn subjugated and the slave worshiped
>
> Do not buy a slave unless he comes with a stick,
> for slaves are surely filthy nuisances
> I never thought I would live to a time
> when a dog would ill-treat me, while being praised.
>
> (W., 691–695)

Once well out of Egypt, al-Mutanabbi resuscitates his heroic self-image in a poem ("Verily every woman sashaying …") that continues the stream of insults against Kafur:

> Before knowing the eunuch, I thought
> that the head was the seat of understanding
> But when I saw his mind [at work]
> I realized that brains are in the testicles
>
> Oh how much poetry I praised that rhinoceros with –
> part poetry, part magical spell [to coax money from him]

All that was not so much panegyric to him
as mockery of mankind.

(W., 699–704)

HOME AGAIN

Although he went to great expense to find al-Mutanabbi, Kafur was unable to capture him. In April, 962, after months crossing the Arabian peninsula, al-Mutanabbi arrived in Kufa, which he had not seen for over thirty years. Ravaged by years of Bedouin raids and Qarmatian rebellion, the poet's home town had little to offer but memories, and at the end of the year al-Mutanabbi left for Baghdad.

Al-Mutanabbi was grandly received in the caliphal capital by rich merchants and scholars, but his welcome by those in power, the Buyids, was anything but warm. The Buyid empire was a confederation of states under the rulership of the Buyid family, who came from Daylam in the southern Caspian. Eventually, the three founding brothers of the dynasty came to control the most important areas once ruled by the Abbasid caliphal government. Not only the sultans, but also their (often more educated and literate) viziers, maintained courts that were active centers of Arab culture and letters. Although the Buyids favored some aspects of indigenous Iranian culture – employing, for example, ancient Iranian titles – Arabic remained the heart of both elite culture and communal religious identity.

Mu'izz al-Dawlah, the Buyid ruler of Baghdad, held a grudge against al-Mutanabbi for panegyrizing his longtime foe, Sayf al-Dawlah, and al-Mutanabbi managed, through his boastful arrogance, to alienate a powerful potential supporter, the sultan's chief minister, al-Hasan ibn Muhammad al-Muhallabi. Given the brilliance of al-Muhallabi's court, which boasted not only diverse men of letters but also a lively taste for the good life, the vizier's hostility to al-Mutanabbi was a serious handicap. Among the literati at al-Muhallabi's court were several who became arch-enemies of al-Mutanabbi, including the polymath and encyclopedist, Abu'l-Faraj al-Isfahani, author of the voluminous *Book of Songs*; the poet, Ibn Hajjaj, who composed coarse insult poetry against al-Mutanabbi; and the poet and rhetorician, Abu 'Ali Muhammad ibn al-Hasan al-Hatimi.

Al-Hatimi turned out to be particularly troublesome. There are different accounts of al-Mutanabbi's tense encounters with al-Muhallabi and the scholars attached to his court. Various versions have it that the poet offended the chief minister by failing to recite an ode to him after his initial warm reception at court; that he on one occasion was engaged in debate at al-Muhallabi's court by Abu'l-Faraj al-Isfahani; that al-Hatimi challenged the poet, first at his residence in front of students attending his lectures, then on three other occasions at the court of al-Muhallabi; that al-Muhallabi and a number of his scholar cohorts formed a cabal dedicated to putting al-Mutanabbi in his place and driving him out of Baghdad, or that the poet ultimately left the "City of Peace" because of the unrelenting abuse from al-Muhallabi's camp. While it is impossible to verify the veracity of these claims, it is certain that al-Mutanabbi's arrogance – and probably his relationship with Sayf al-Dawlah – irritated the vizier and his associates, and that al-Hatimi did successfully challenge the poet publicly on at least one occasion (Bonebakker, 42; 52) by pointing out verses of his poetry that he claimed were plagiarized and testing him on poetry, philology, and lexicography.

While the report of al-Hatimi's thrashing of al-Mutanabbi undoubtedly pleased the vizier, and perhaps even the sultan, it is doubtful whether the hostile conspiracy against him was so elaborate and sustained as some sources suggest. It is probable that the debate between al-Mutanabbi and al-Hatimi, which involved rude behavior and speech on the part of both, ended with the two scholars on amicable terms, given the fact that al-Hatimi is known later to have attended al-Mutanabbi's study circle. While it is true that by then al-Mutanabbi's fame and following were extensive, given the animosity of al-Hatimi's patron, al-Muhallabi, toward al-Mutanabbi, it is unlikely that anything but a measure of real admiration could have moved al-Hatimi to praise and even study with the poet.

Al-Mutanabbi was sustained during his time in Baghdad by wealthy businessmen outside the main circles of political power, who provided a base of support from which he was able to attend to the meticulous collection of his poetry. Figures who were to play a pivotal role in disseminating and explicating his *diwan*, such as Ibn Jinni, his old supporter from Aleppo, joined his entourage. Admirers and students recorded verse from the poet's youth which he recited at Baghdad, and even preserved compositions that the author had purged from his collection.

Whether because of al-Muhallabi and company or some other reason, al-Mutanabbi left Baghdad in August, 963 to return to Kufa. Shortly after the poet's return to his natal city, the Qarmatian uprising resumed in and around Kufa, under the leadership of a Bedouin, Dabba ibn Yazid al-'Utbi. When Dabba remained unmoved by the obscene invective al-Mutanabbi composed against him at the urging of the city leaders, and the raids against the poet's home town continued, al-Mutanabbi participated in the battle that turned back the rebels. As reward, the sultan Mu'izz al-Dawlah's general sent al-Mutanabbi a cloak and the poet responded with an ode of thanks. At this point, the dual features of al-Mutanabbi's self-image – poet and warrior – came together more harmoniously and heroically than at perhaps any other time in his life.

SAYF AL-DAWLAH IN THE WINGS

Al-Mutanabbi never completely lost contact with his former patron, Sayf al-Dawlah. The figure of the Hamdanid prince served as a leitmotif in al-Mutanabbi's poetry from the time he left Aleppo – here appearing as the yearned-for friend and protector he regretted leaving, there as the ingrate who had responded with cruelty to the poet's loyalty and affection. At some points al-Mutanabbi declared his fierce independence; at others he betrayed a hope of rejoining Sayf al-Dawlah.

Sayf al-Dawlah seems to have held on to the ambition of luring his favorite poet back to Aleppo. While al-Mutanabbi was in

Kufa – during either the first or second visit there since fleeing Egypt – Sayf al-Dawlah sent him a present of robes and money, to which al-Mutanabbi responded with a poem of thanks ("What's wrong with us, O messenger …"). In this poem, Sayf al-Dawlah is praised for his generosity and his bravery in battle, as poetic convention demanded. Al-Mutanabbi establishes a clear hierarchy among leaders and patrons, unequivocally placing Sayf al-Dawlah at the top. At certain points, he suggests that he might wish to return to Aleppo, but the poem ends (v. 42) on a note of resignation, with an implication that the separation may continue. Although the conclusion has a ring of real affection, the poem is for the most part formal and predictable, without the clear tone of intimacy that characterized many of his earlier odes to Sayf al-Dawlah:

> Whenever the gardens welcomed us, we said:
> Aleppo is our destination, you are [merely] the path
>
> Many are those named "prince,"
> but the one there [in Aleppo] is the one hoped for
> The one I left to travel east and west
> while his generosity remains before me, never diminishing
>
> Oh, 'Ali, there is no hero but you
> whose sword is drawn to protect his honor
> How could Iraq and Egypt not be secure
> when your troops and horses guard them
>
> I am not content that you be generous
> while fate is stingy about my seeing you
> Distance from you has spoiled the nearness of your gifts
> My pasture is abundant, but my body is emaciated
>
> As long as you are alive, I have one thousand Kafurs among
> my slaves
> and a countryside and a Nile from your generosity
> I would not care whom fate's perversities struck and its disasters
> claimed,
> so long as calamity shielded you.
>
> (W., 613–618)

When Sayf al-Dawlah's older sister, Khawlah, died, al-Mutanabbi sent him an elegy in her honor ("Oh, sister of the best of brothers ...," W., 607–613). This poem, in honor of the remaining sister of al-Mutanabbi's erstwhile patron and friend, reveals little of the depth of feeling and psychological insight that characterized his earlier elegies on Sayf al-Dawlah's family members. Death is blamed for having betrayed Sayf al-Dawlah, who had so often done its bidding by bringing death to his enemies in battle (v. 5). The dead woman is first described in terms normally used to eulogize men, with the declaration that her passing brought death to many and silenced the uproar of armies in battle (v. 4). Once affirmed, her femaleness is regretted, qualified, and all but denied, as she is portrayed as a special kind of woman – a woman in spite of herself. Unlike other women, preoccupied with amusement and recreation, she is concerned with acquiring glory (v. 15). She may look beautiful, but no one but God realizes how sharp are her teeth behind her beautiful smile (v. 16). "The part of her hair causes happiness in the hearts of perfume / and regret in the hearts of helmets and leather shields" (v. 17) because she does not don them, as they would like. Finally, the poet declares outright:

> Though she was created female, she was created
> noble, unlike a woman in mind and quality.
>
> (W., 609)

The poet redeems the hyperbole of his praise by affirming that her excellence is unique, superior even to the merits of her tribe – "there is a quality to wine that does not exist in the grape" (v. 20) – and concluding that no one, man or woman, can compare to her (v. 23). Some scholars have fancied al-Mutanabbi to have been in love with Khawlah, the subject of this elegy. This poem would be a sad testament if that were the case, given its compulsive denial of Khawlah's femaleness.

We know next to nothing about the poet's love-life. In al-Mutanabbi's *oeuvre*, *ghazal* (love poetry), most of it occurring in the introductions to some seventy odes, is extremely limited in quantity and is open to differing interpretations. The only point about which there is agreement in this connection is that al-Mutanabbi excelled in his description of Bedouin women, for whom he expressed a preference over city women. In the ode on Khawlah, the dead woman has little actual presence; indeed the most compelling feminine presence – in the form of both feminine singular and feminine plural referents – is that of "the days" or "the nights," the temporal vehicles of fate. Out of the landscape of gender ambiguity, indeed competition, created by the verses described above, emerges the strong, consistent, grammatically feminine voice of fate. In an apostrophe to Sayf al-Dawlah, the poet prays the nights never catch up with him, since they are capable of defeating even the strongest person with even the weakest of instruments. Four verses trumpet the perfidy and inescapability of fate, and then after two verses of the type that might have invited accusations of theological impropriety, in which he signals the existence of ongoing debate about whether or not the soul survives death, the poet declares the uselessness of that kind of speculation:

> Whoever speculates on the world and his soul
> will be left by contemplation between impotence and weariness.
>
> (v. 44, W., 613)

There is none of the resuscitation of Sayf al-Dawlah's heroic persona or rebuilding of his wounded psyche of the type we saw in the poet's earlier elegies. In this poem, the aggrieved Sayf al-Dawlah is left defeated – defeated by the one solidly female element in the poem, the nights. The rationale of the earlier part of the poem, with its denigration of femaleness, becomes also the basis of a virtual emasculation of Sayf al-Dawlah, as the aphoristic, cerebral ending of the poem starkly leaves the bereaved brother with nothing but "impotence." This may simply be the voice of an older, more pessimistic poet, or it may be evidence of his diminished attachment to or even continued bitterness toward Sayf al-Dawlah. In any case, the detachment, even coldness, of this poem argues against the idea that al-Mutanabbi was deeply interested in rejoining Sayf al-Dawlah at his court in Aleppo.

Finally, in late 964, the Hamdanid wrote to al-Mutanabbi explicitly inviting him back to his court. Al-Mutanabbi responded with a forty-four-line poem ("I understand your letter …,"W., 618–623). Though the poem is full of declarations of loyalty to Sayf al-Dawlah and insistence on the prince's unequivocal superiority over all other kings and patrons – ("If I called them by his name [i.e. 'sword']/still, he is of iron and they are wooden," W., 619) – the poet seems to be keeping his options open for the future:

> I understand your letter – the kindest of missives
> [I say] to the prince of the Arabs: I hear
> and obey, delighted with him,
> though action falls short of what is required.
>
> (W., 618)

Circumstances – and probably al-Mutanabbi's shrewd assessment of them – kept the two men apart. Sayf al-Dawlah's increasing physical frailty and his intermittent political vulnerability must have made the prince's invitation less enticing than it might otherwise have been. Al-Mutanabbi did not set out for Aleppo. Ironically, it was a non-Arab, culturally different environment that would claim the last stage of this chauvinistically Arab poet's creativity and life.

THE POET IN PERSIA

So great had al-Mutanabbi's fame become that he was by now well known throughout the Muslim world. Toward the end of 963, al-Mutanabbi had received an invitation to Arrajan from the Buyid vizier, Abu'l Fadl Muhammad Ibn al-'Amid. Ibn al-'Amid (d. 970 CE), whose name became synonymous with excellent prose style for centuries after his death, was one of the most outstanding among a group of highly literate Buyid viziers who assiduously encouraged intellectual exchange at their influential courts. His erudition was not limited to prose and poetry; he was also well versed in mathematics and the physical sciences. The vizier was known to be as generous a patron as Sayf al-Dawlah, and probably more indulgent of the poets at his court. He was also known, however, for his envy of al-Mutanabbi, which led him to avoid talking about him or listening to his poetry. According to one anecdote, a friend paying a visit found Ibn al-'Amid despondent. The visitor was surprised to learn that the cause of his unhappiness was not the recent death of his sister, as he had assumed, but rather the vizier's continuing vexation with al-Mutanabbi:

> This Mutanabbi matter and my effort to suppress mention of him is annoying me: I've received some sixty letters of condolence and every one begins with [two verses from al-Mutanabbi's elegy on Sayf al-Dawlah's sister]. How can I possibly stifle his reputation?
>
> *al-Subh al-munabbi*, 146–147

In January, 965, al-Mutanabbi left Kufa for Arrajan with his son, Muhassad, and a number of his close protégés, including Ibn Jinni and his staunchest supporter from Baghdad, 'Ali al-Basri. The poet was grandly received in Persia and for three months he lived luxuriously in a fine residence. Reassured that he would be neither ignored nor insulted by this powerful poet, Ibn al-'Amid rewarded al-Mutanabbi generously for his panegyrics. Treated as a star at the scholarly discussions that took place at the vizier's assemblies, al-Mutanabbi found Ibn al-'Amid and his entourage lively and critical interlocutors.

Of the three odes that he composed for his Persian patron, the first ("Your love is apparent …") was a remake of a poem originally intended for an Ikhshidid vizier in Egypt, which he never actually recited. The ode begins with a detailed departure scene, as typically occurred in the prelude of pre-Islamic and early Islamic odes. The poet moves from this lengthy (thirteen verses) opening to a description of his arduous passage to the patron's domain – also a standard component of panegyric poetry – with a verse meant to testify to the deliberateness of his choice to join Ibn al-'Amid's court: "Time gave, but I did not accept its gift / It had intentions for me, but I wanted to choose" (W., 734). After several lines of praise for Ibn al-'Amid's military skill, the poet pays tribute to his patron's erudition and eloquence:

> Other men pluck words before they're sprouted,
> but you pluck words when they bloom
> So when they pass from your mouth, men's ears follow them,
> and their beauty is multiplied when they are repeated
> When you are silent, the most eloquent preacher
> is a pen that has taken your fingers as a pulpit
> and epistles whose binding enemies cut
> to find lances, the points of swords, and armor.
>
> (W., 736–737)

Al-Mutanabbi then brings the contrast between his native, Arab culture and formation and the Persian identity and environment of his new patron into relief, declaring a preference for the latter. He claims that Ibn al-'Amid encompasses all that Bedouin culture had to offer, and surpasses it, being, like Ptolemy, "at once king, Bedouin and city-dweller:"

> Who will inform the desert Arabs that after them I
> have seen Aristotle and Alexander?
> I tired of slaughtering she-camels, so I was entertained
> by one who sacrifices bags of gold for those he hosts
> And I heard Ptolemy studying his books,
> at once king, Bedouin and city-dweller,
> And I met [in him] all the men of learning, as if
> God had restored their souls and their eras.
>
> (W., 738–739)

At the end of the poem, the poet summons up the grief of the prototypically Arab departure scene evoked at the beginning of the poem, now in the person of the "real" woman weeping at the poet's departure to the court of Ibn al-'Amid at Arrajan: "Would that the weeping woman whose tears grieved me / could look on you as I have, so she would forgive me" (W., 739). As if to defend his choice of a Persian abode and deny any conflict between his Arab and Persian homes, he declares that the weeping woman "Would see one virtue not opposing another / with the sun shining while the clouds are as big as mountains" (W., 739). Listing the conventionally recognized parts of the Arabic ode – the amatory prelude that includes the lingering at the abode of a lost love, and the arduous journey to the patron being praised – the poet simultaneously boasts of the excellence of his poetry and makes a performative statement about the outcome of his new employment: "Of all people, I have the nicest abode / am happiest with my mount, and have the most profitable merchandise" (W., 740). In this way, his new patron, Ibn al-'Amid, is represented as the antidote to the pathos of the elegiac prelude of the conventional Arabic ode.

This poem was followed by one composed on the occasion of the feast of Noruz in March, 965, and then several weeks later by a farewell poem to Ibn al-'Amid. Al-Mutanabbi decided to accept an invitation from the Buyid sultan, 'Adud al-Dawlah – son of the second of the three founding brothers of the Buyid dynasty and pupil of Ibn al-'Amid – to join his court at Shiraz. There, al-Mutanabbi was received in a manner befitting a celebrity by a patron who was known for the breadth of his culture, the extent of his power, and the brilliance of his court. In Shiraz, even his former enemy from the days in Aleppo, the philologist, Abu 'Ali al-Farisi, had to acknowledge al-Mutanabbi's excellence and his importance.

THE GAP OF BAVVAN

Of the handful of odes – panegyrics and elegies – that al-Mutanabbi composed during his stay in Shiraz, two stand out as expanding the limits of not only the poet's *oeuvre*, but also the canonical focus of pre-modern Arabic poetry. The first is a poem about the splendors of the Gap of Bavvan ("Bawwan" in Arabic). This glade, outside the city of Shiraz, which the poet passed through on his way to the court of 'Adud al-Dawlah, was renowned for its abundant trees and water, and was considered by some contemporary geographers to be among the four garden paradises of the world. The first eighteen lines of the poem are:

> Because of their pleasantness the abodes of the glade are to dwelling-places
> what spring is to the times of the year
> But an Arab man there is
> a stranger in face, hand, and tongue
> Playgrounds to jinn, if Solomon roamed there
> he would take along an interpreter
> They so beckoned our horsemen and the horses that
> I feared, despite their nobility, that they would become refractory
> We went forth in the morning, with the branches shaking
> silver beads like pearls on their manes
> I proceeded, the branches having blocked the sun from me
> and allowed in just enough light for me
> The light entering through the chinks between the branches cast dinars
> on my clothing that eluded my fingertips
> They have fruit that make you think of
> glasses of wine standing there without containers
> And streams that make their pebbles clink
> like jewelry on the hands of singing-girls
> If this were Damascus, my reins would be diverted
> by someone with kettles white as china, skilled at making *tharid* stew,
> who uses aloe wood to kindle a fire for guests,
> whose smoke is fragrant with perfume
> You dwell with him with a brave heart
> and depart from him with a timorous one
> [They are] abodes of which a specter remains
> accompanying me to Nawbandajan
> When the ash-colored pigeons sing there
> the songs of the singing-girls answer them back
> And those in the glade are more in need of explication
> than singing and cooing pigeons
> The two descriptions may seem similar,
> but the two described are far apart
> In the glade of Bawwan my horse said:
> would you lead me away from this to battling with lances?

Your father, Adam, set the model for defiance
and taught you about leaving gardens.

(W., 766–769)

This poem is remarkable not only because of the lyricism of this opening movement and the sensual immediacy of its description of the natural environment, but also because of the key role played in it by the psychology of the poetic persona. There is a clear tension between Arab and Persian culture, which results in verses that sometimes verge on being disrespectful to the latter. What salvages deference in the face of the bold tone of such verses is that this tension is presented as the personal dilemma and conflict – even the shortcoming – of the poet's persona. The initial section of the poem thus eschews the often static quality of many panegyric poems and presents a dynamically evolving psychological process and a more dynamic treatment of nature than is customary in the medieval Arabic poetic tradition.

The diction of the very first verse of this poem – words such as "dwelling-places/abodes" – summons up the prelude of the classical Arabic ode. Here, though, the hyperbolic praise of the Persian abodes that are the focus of the piece makes clear that this is not the abandoned abode of the Arabic tradition; this is the most fertile and lush of gardens – like spring among the seasons, when the world comes to life and everything seems hopeful and positive. The contrast between the Persian environment and the archetypal Arab one is thus erected from the opening moments of the poem – to the benefit of the Persian. Very quickly, the poet raises the stakes, by giving this contrast between the two cultures a personal aspect: this may be the most beautiful of environments, but the Arab's sense of strangeness here is complete. This verse (v. 2) brings the poet's persona – alluded to in the phrase, "the Arab man" – into the mix and establishes it as the prism through which all that follows is to be interpreted. Without this personal perspective, the next and later verses might come across as unacceptably dismissive of things Persian. "Playgrounds to jinn, if Solomon roamed there/he would take along an interpreter"

(v. 3). This is a reference to the Qur'anic verse that describes Solomon as understanding all languages, which allows him to keep men, jinn, and birds in order (27:16–17). Although, as the Arab commentators point out, referring to the Persians as "jinn" can be complimentary, the stark exaggeration of the otherness of the Persians and their language seems rather bold, given the fact that the poem is supposed to be a panegyric to a new, Persian patron.

Al-Mutanabbi was the standard-bearer for the dominant Arab culture, which meant that his emphasis on the foreignness of his Buyid hosts implied inferiority on their part. But in the context of the poet's personal psychological predicament – his lonely sense of being an alien in this new land – the verse comes across as less offensive. The emotional state of the poet has become the rudder of the poem, the arbiter of what is acceptable. In a poetic mode – panegyric – severely limited by the dictates of both tradition and social propriety, al-Mutanabbi managed to transfer a large measure of discriminatory authority to the voice of his persona. Indeed, al-Mutanabbi's vulnerability serves the eulogistic function of the poem. He was in a Persian environment, and this quintessentially Arab poet's admission to being so completely at a loss there served to exaggerate the reality that the actual, rather than the symbolic, holders of political power in the region were non-Arab. The prestige of the Buyid court may have required partaking in and encouraging the ascendancy of Arabic arts and letters, but the place, the language, and the local identity were Persian.

The next six lines of the poem are an exquisite description of the poet's experience of the beauty of the glade. The images employed here are compelling in their sensuality. All the senses are called upon in the metaphors of these verses: the feel of the water sprinkled from the tree branches as the riders pass under them, the light of the sun that flickers in between the branches, and the streams that gurgle. Touch and sight coalesce in the image of illusory dinars, made of light, that evade the rider's touch. Even taste is suggested in the image of fleshy, juicy, colorful fruits dangling from the branches. This verse, attributed by some to al-Mutanabbi's predecessors, al-Buhturi and Abu Tammam, is transplanted from its original, bacchic context to a description of nature.

This paean to the beauty of the region is compelling not just because of the sensual immediacy and comprehensive evocativeness of its images, but also because of how it is folded into the dominant note of the poem, the poet's state of mind. In these lines, the beauty of the glade is represented as having so primal a power that even the well-trained horses are tempted to stop and linger. Nature is described as being protective of the newcomer passing through, guiding him through the unfamiliar terrain. The branches shield him from the sun, but allow in enough light to make his passage possible. It is even playful, as it paints coins of light on his clothing through the tree covering. The poet is not entirely in control, but rather has had to yield gratefully to a benevolent natural environment. He sees where he is going, but barely – this when he has no experience of the area to tell him what to expect. The reader has the sense of a rider very tentatively discovering the wonders around him bit by bit, as the elements permit. Senses alert to the unknown, the poet conveys both the vulnerability and exhilaration that comes with the experience of unfamiliar beauty.

Next, the poet conjures up a scene of Arab hospitality in Damascus, the natural beauty of which would be recognized as a worthy rival to the Gap of Bavvan. Were this Damascus, the poet would be stopped by an Arab brother eager to shower him with unstinting hospitality. The scene has a strongly Bedouin flavor. The reference to kettles that are as white as china derives from a well-known metaphor for a generous man, in whose kettles can be seen the white hump of the camel cooking in the stew. The owner does not just feed his guests some weak stew, but slaughters a camel to enrich it. This familiar scene of Arab hospitality serves to emphasize the poet's sense of insecurity in his new, Persian environment. If this were Damascus, he would know what to expect; not so, here, in this Persian garden. There, the poet would linger, safe and confident, not timid as he is *en route* to Shiraz. With this scene, replete with tropes that resonate from the Bedouin Arab origins of Arabic poetry, the contrast between the familiar Arab cultural environment and the unknown, if appealing, Persian environment is brought into stark relief. This image of Arab abodes remains with him on his way to the Buyid court at Shiraz, providing an emotional security that is otherwise lacking.

The poet's equivocal response to the valley of Bavvan is signalled by its pigeons, which both sing and coo, indicating joy and sadness. Two Arabic words that mean "dwelling-places" or "abodes" are used to refer both to the glade and to Arab abodes, implying that the Persian and the Arab locales are meant to be contrasted. The basic emotional dilemma signalled in the second line of the poem is thus propelled toward some resolution. By line 15, the poet's uncertainty remains, in his inability to interpret the sounds of the pigeons and his emphasis on the incomprehensibility of the people of the Gap of Bavvan. Here again is a line that could cause offense, were it not deeply embedded in the poet's psychology, as laid out for us up to this point in the poem. With the poet's ambivalence and insecurity only partly resolved, the patron appears on the scene in the panegyric section of the poem to represent the only possible means of true resolution and peace for the poet. This is conveyed in lines 19 and 20:

> I said: When I see Abu Shuja'
> I forget about everyone else and this place
> For people and the world are [but] a road
> to one who has no match among men.

(W., 769)

These two lines are familiar formulae, with nothing unique about them in the context of Arabic panegyric poetry. What makes them new, what gives them a measure of emotional power, is what came before them in the eighteen lines leading up to the panegyric. By way of capping this, the poet dismisses his earlier patrons as mere training tools with which he readied himself for the one worthy patron, 'Adud al-Dawlah:

I trained myself in poetry on them,
just as one first learns to charge with a lance that has no point.

(W., 769)

Most of what follows in the praise section of the poem is familiar fare. Al-Mutanabbi praises 'Adud al-Dawlah for the peace and security he has created in his realm, and his two sons as two chips off his exalted lineal block. Certain lines, such as one in which he likens 'Adud al-Dawlah to a fine Yemeni sword and his poetry to the embellishment on it (v. 47), might well have been composed earlier with Sayf al-Dawlah in mind, given al-Mutanabbi's fondness for metaphors that played on his name, "sword of the state." But in the first half of the poem, al-Mutanabbi found a way to breathe life into the hackneyed motifs of pre-modern praise poetry. Through the portrait of his vulnerability and insecurity that is played out in relation to the natural beauty of the Persian land, with Arab culture and tradition as contrast, the poet set up the need for a hero; opened a gap for the patron-hero to step into. It is not uncommon in 'Abbasid poetry for the poet to attempt to establish his need for the goodwill and generosity of the patron, in the hope of encouraging him to reward the poet well. What is impressive about this poem is that the need the poet paints is an emotional one, and the patron is presented as the only one who can fulfill it. The patron, set up poetically to trump his Arab predecessors in generosity and solicitude for the poet, would thus secure the sought-after imprimatur of al-Mutanabbi, icon of Arab elite culture.

TO THE HUNT

In another rare departure from his familiar poetic fare, in July, 965 al-Mutanabbi composed a poem describing a hunting expedition that his patron, 'Adud al-Dawlah, conducted following the successful routing of a Kurdish tribe. With his army in tow, 'Adud al-Dawlah rode on an elephant to the plain of Dasht al-Arzan, and while there he asked al-Mutanabbi, who was also a participant in the hunt, to write a poem describing the event.

This long poem – 118 half-lines – is in the "quick" meter, which creates a brisk pace, befitting the scene. It contains some descriptions of the birds and animals being hunted which are reminiscent of the kind typically found in hunt poems, such as the description of the ibex as having "black beards with no mustaches" (v. 31, al-Wahidi's numbering) which, when loosened, resemble nets in which corrupt judges try to snare the wealth of orphaned children (v. 34–35). Overall, however, it is very different from the hunt poems of al-Mutanabbi's much admired predecessor, Abu Nuwas, and the famous 137-line hunt narrative of his arch-rival, Abu Firas al-Hamdani, cousin of Sayf al-Dawlah. Unlike the monothematic hunting poems of an earlier period, which in al-Mutanabbi's day were largely out of fashion, this piece, after its initial boast, joins panegyric to the features of the hunt. Reference to the preceding military campaign merges seamlessly into the hunt scene, so that the hunt comes across as simply another type of battle, just as compelling a proof of the patron's dominance and superiority as his military prowess.

The emphasis on the self-importance of 'Adud al-Dawlah and the haughtiness of his army's entry on to the site of the hunt renders these verses subtly parodic. Given the manpower 'Adud al-Dawlah had at his disposal, and the elaborateness of his entourage, the hyperbole of the panegyric verges on the ridiculous. As if fearing that the vast assortment of animals on the site was not complete, 'Adud al-Dawlah, we are told, adds an elephant (v. 22). So renowned is he for his hunting skills that even the beasts of Najd, on the Arabian peninsula, fear him (v. 43). They even wish that 'Adud al-Dawlah would send them a governor to subjugate them, thus sparing them the terror of being hunted (v. 48). The poet tells his patron: "There is nothing left for you but to hunt ogres / in the dark, moonless nights" (W., 799). Even the final, customary reference to the patron's noble lineage has a hint of mockery of the well-known pomp and elaborate attire of Persian rulers, which is often contrasted in Abbasid poetry with the rough-and-ready Arab Bedouin mien:

Oh, arm of the state and of glorious deeds,
lineage is the true embellishment and you are adorned
by your father, not by earrings and anklets,
as he is adorned by your excellence.

(W., 799)

FINAL CALL

Despite the respect and luxury al-Mutanabbi enjoyed at the court of Shiraz, his attachment to things Arab left him feeling alien in an essentially Persian environment. This feeling of loneliness and of being "a stranger in face, hand, and tongue" precluded an extended stay in Iranian lands, and in August, 965 the poet requested and received 'Adud al-Dawlah's permission to leave Shiraz, though perhaps not permanently. Al-Mutanabbi composed an ode in farewell ("May he who falls short …").

As fate would have it, this was to be al-Mutanabbi's last poem. On his way to Baghdad – perhaps ultimately headed for Syria – he stopped in Wasit with his son, al-Muhassad, and Ali al-Basri and his entourage. During his stay in Wasit, al-Mutanabbi learned that among the Bedouins who were raiding the region at that time was Fatik ibn Abi al-Jahl, the uncle of Dabba Ibn Yazid al-'Utbi whom al-Mutanabbi had satirized during the Kufa rebellions the year before. Although the poet was warned that Fatik had made clear his intention to avenge his nephew's honor by killing al-Mutanabbi and helping himself to the poet's ample possessions, al-Mutanabbi refused the escort judiciously offered by his anxious host. In September, 965 the poet and his small group of intimates were attacked by Fatik's band. Outnumbered, al-Mutanabbi, his son, and a number of his servants died. The attackers took his money and possessions, and what wasn't stolen was scattered, including the notebooks containing his edited poems. Various reports circulated regarding this final battle of al-Mutanabbi's. According to one, the poet, after fiercely battling his attackers, was on the verge of fleeing when he was coaxed back into action by one of his slaves, who quoted a line of pure bravado from his poetry: "What happened to that verse of yours – 'The horses and the night and the barren desert know me/so too, war and combat and paper and pen'?" (*al-Subh al-munabbi*, 175). Dead at fifty years of age, al-Mutanabbi was elegized by poets throughout the Islamic world, which he had graced since youth with his art and challenged, for better or worse, with his provocative presence. In his elegy on the poet, al-Mutanabbi's devoted student, Ibn Jinni, expressed the view of his many admirers when he said:

> Poetry has sunk into the earth and the bloom of literature withered, and the lush tree of letters, once abundantly watered, has dried up.

5

CONTEMPORARY CRITICS

AFTER THE FALL

Al-Mutanabbi's fame, and his activities as teacher, conserver, and interpreter of his poetry, guaranteed the wide dissemination and continued interest in his *diwan* after his death. Everywhere he composed poetry, from Aleppo to Shiraz, and especially in Baghdad, there formed study circles frequented by ardent admirers and students, who carefully noted the master's comments and recitations and took his poetry back to their home communities and abroad. Thanks to the organizing and editing al-Mutanabbi undertook during the difficult days of his final stay in Baghdad, the poet left the world with a chronologically organized *diwan*. His efforts to purge the collection of poems he no longer deemed worthy of him were thwarted by students who recorded every recollected piece, whether or not the poet wished them discarded.

After his death, his devoted students and protégés recited and transmitted the poetry, along with the author's comments and explanations. 'Ali ibn Hamzah al-Basri, who had so valiantly sustained the poet in the face of official rejection in Baghdad, became the first to collect the poet's *diwan* and became a key transmitter of his work. In Egypt, after al-Mutanabbi's departure, the leadership of his seminar passed to the chancellery secretary, Salih ibn Rushdayn. The early commentary by Ibn Jinni, the loyal student and admirer whom al-Mutanabbi had referred to as "our friend," became a key source for the many commentaries that were to follow. Reporting comments by the poet himself and anecdotes about him on the authority of al-Basri, Ibn Jinni represented an important direct link to the poet and his preferences.

However, al-Mutanabbi had made many enemies during his life and his poetry had many determined detractors. During his lifetime, and in the century following his death, a number of critical treatises were produced which engendered many responses and defenses. Much of this material has not survived. For example, the poet Abu'l-'Abbas al-Nami (d. 1008 CE), whose position at the court of Aleppo al-Mutanabbi usurped, is said to have produced a treatise about al-Mutanabbi's faults which, along with much of the Aleppan critical legacy, is lost. In this chapter we will examine the main issues and approaches adopted in some of the principal critical treatises that undertook to evaluate al-Mutanabbi's work.

LINGUISTIC CORRECTNESS

Medieval Arabic literary theory traditionally focused to a great extent on the correct use of the Arabic language. The critics and poets who undertook to find fault with al-Mutanabbi's poetry quite naturally followed this pattern and produced works focusing on linguistic details, such as grammatical correctness.

One of the earliest was the Egyptian poet, Abu Muhammad al-Hasan Ibn Waki al-Tinnisi (d. 1003 CE), who, like his Aleppan colleague, al-Nami, seems to have been moved by more than a little envy of al-Mutanabbi's talent and official recognition. Somewhat more methodical and comprehensive in his treatment of the poetry than many of his successors in the anti-Mutanabbi party, Ibn Waki' undertook to provide a critical assessment of al-Mutanabbi's entire *diwan*, poem by poem. The result is his *The Fair Way in Judging Poetry and Exposing the Plagiarisms of al-Mutanabbi and that which is Dubious in His Poetry*. It is clear from quotations that have survived in al-'Ukbari's commentary on the *diwan* that the version of this work that has come down to us is incomplete. None the less, in addition to its two theoretical presentations of the issues relating to plagiarism – a subject to which we will return shortly – and rhetorical figures, it provides a valuable example of early Arabic practical criticism. The overall opinion of al-Mutanabbi that Ibn Waki' presents is that, while the poet is undeniably excellent, he does not deserve to be given precedence over earlier poets who were superior to him, such as Abu Tammam and al-Buhturi.

Ibn Waki' and others found fault with al-Mutanabbi in linguistic details such as the omission of the vocative particle in a particular verse, the vocalization of individual words (such as making quiescent a consonant that should be vocalized), the excessive use of demonstrative pronouns and adjectives, and the use of particular plural formations of certain nouns. This trend – along with many of the same examples – was taken up by many later critics eager to find al-Mutanabbi less than the consummate crafter of poetry he and his advocates claimed he was. It was apparently the claims of poetic superiority made by the poet and his supporters that seem to have most piqued his critics and inspired their meticulous search for weaknesses in his poetry.

The mechanics of the formal features of poetry, including meter and rhyme, were more rarely focused on in negative considerations of al-Mutanabbi's poetry, but Ibn Waki' found fault even there, though he did not go so far as others who claimed that al-Mutanabbi deliberately made use of difficult meters just to show off his mastery of Arabic prosody.

DICTION AND LEXICAL CHOICE

One repeated complaint about al-Mutanabbi's poetry was the low style it sometimes manifested as a result of his use of colloquial vocabulary or vulgarisms. Al-Tha'alibi (d. 1038 CE), the literary critic and biographer who dedicated a lengthy chapter to al-Mutanabbi in his rich anthology, *The Matchless Pearl of the Ages*, lists a number of verses that illustrate this vice. All things considered, al-Tha'alibi was one of al-Mutanabbi's more even-handed critics, for in his chapter on the poet he included not only the blameworthy aspects of his work, but also separate and extensive coverage of its admirable features. The expert anthologist's concern with thoroughness and complete coverage of all the critical objections in circulation about al-Mutanabbi's poetry is evident, for his list includes a number of verses composed in the poet's youth, along with several lines of invective against Dabba. The bad taste of youth, one would have thought, might have been forgiven, not to mention the coarse vocabulary that was entirely in keeping with the established norms for Arabic insult poetry. In both cases the vulgarity is clear. What is offensive about other verses included is less obvious, as in the following two verses from an encomium to Abu'l-Husayn 'Ali ibn Ahmad al-Khurasani:

> Some poetry is raving,
> worth nothing, while some is wisdom
> Among it is that which is obtained by skill and
> excellence, and that which is caused by delirium.
>
> (W., 250–251)

The obvious boast on the part of al-Mutanabbi, coupled with his undisguised contempt for other poets, is hardly unusual in his *oeuvre*, and al-Tha'alibi would have had to cite many more verses if that were what he found offensive. It may have been the explicit mention of the "hot tumor," said to cause delirium, that some critics found distasteful. We can only imagine that the mention of the disease summoned up nastier associations than now seem apparent. Perhaps the pairing of this unpleasant reference with an idea that derives from a prophetic saying ("Verily there is poetry that is wisdom") inspired the rejection.

This last example conveys the tone of much of the criticism of al-Mutanabbi, and especially that of al-Sahib ibn 'Abbad (d. 995 CE), the Buyid vizier and renowned prose writer and poet who never forgave the poet for snubbing him when he was a young man. As the story goes, the young al-Sahib ibn 'Abbad was keen to be panegyrized by the acknowledged star in the field and wrote to al-Mutanabbi promising to give him half of all his wealth if he would join him in Isfahan. When he did not deign to respond to Ibn 'Abbad's request, the ever-diplomatic al-Mutanabbi made a lasting enemy; and of a man who was to become one of the most important literary patrons of his era. The animus behind Ibn 'Abbad's treatment of the poet is clear throughout his treatise, *Uncovering the Shortcomings in al-Mutanabbi's Poetry*. He even goes so far as to find fault with the poet for using non-Arabic words – this, despite the rarity of such items in his work and the fact that many poets before him had occasionally used foreign words.

Finally, al-Mutanabbi was blamed by many for using unusual vocabulary. This was a charge leveled at many "modern" poets, some of whom deserved it far more than al-Mutanabbi, and did not offer a major weapon to those wishing to find fault with his poetry. More serious, in the eyes of some critics, were al-Mutanabbi's sins against propriety, such as using speech that was inappropriate to the context. In the view of some commentators, the following verse from a poem to 'Ali ibn Ibrahim al-Tanukhi was an example of such impropriety, since the lips of princes are not to be envied.

> I envy the glass as it passes
> over the lips of prince Abu 'l-Husayn.

(W., 136)

CONSTRUCTION OF THE POEM

The critical comments cited up to this point have all focused on either individual words or phrases, or on one or two lines of poetry, which was typical of the medieval Arabic literary theorists. None the less, some attention was paid to the way individual poems were put together, for example, in al-Hatimi's criticism of al-Mutanabbi's first panegyric to Kafur ("It is sickness enough ..."), where, in his view, the opening topic did not fit the main theme of the poem. Such discussions most often tended to focus on individual verses that served as points of transitions in the poems – for example, the pivot verse(s) that provided the transition from the amatory prelude to the journey section or the praise or boast section of a poem. On this front, our poet fared well enough. Although there was a relative consensus among the critics about the excellence of al-Mutanabbi's transitions, one of the more fair-minded of his critics did mention several he considered weak. In his *Mediation between al-Mutanabbi and His Opponents*, al-Qadi al-Jurjani (d. 1002 CE) attempted to give full consideration to the various opinions of al-Mutanabbi, pro and con, and to both the poet's weaknesses and strengths, to arrive at a just assessment of the poet's place in Arabic poetry. His overall judgment was that every poet had faults and al-Mutanabbi was no exception yet, al-Mutanabbi had produced an abundance of good poetry and very little that was inferior and his superior poetry was quite sufficient to establish him as a poet of high rank. Although an admirer of al-Mutanabbi, al-Qadi al-Jurjani was zealous about giving all sides a full hearing and often went out of his way to include every negative critique of the poet. In the handful of examples of contrived transitions that al-Qadi al-Jurjani lists – which he allows are not completely condemnable – are the following two from an encomium to Kafur ("I used to wish that white hair …"). Much is implicit in the critics' selection of verses in their discussions of transition: al-Qadi al-Jurjani objects to too sudden a shift from one poetic movement to the next. Here, for example, the sudden mention of the patron without any preparation is too mechanical an entrée to the praise section of the poem, falling short of the seamlessness that was the generally accepted goal:

> The most noble place in the world is the saddle of a fast horse
> and the best companion ever is a book
> Abu'l-Misk is a bountiful sea,
> fuller and more vehemently flowing than any other sea.
>
> (W., 683–684)

PHILOSOPHIZING IN POETRY

Al-Sahib ibn ʿAbbad and others accused the poet of abandoning the language of poetry for that of the logicians and philosophers. The following are examples of the type of verses that occasioned this charge, the first from a poem in praise of Abu'l-ʿAshaʾir, the cousin of Sayf al-Dawlah:

> Sorrow before the soul departs is impotence
> and sorrow does not exist after the parting.
>
> (W., 353)

The transmitter and commentator of al-Mutanabbi's *diwan*, al-ʿArudi (d. 1025 CE), accused al-Mutanabbi of apostasy for this verse, with its expression of the finality of death and man's impotence before it. The starkness of its statement, the bold truth of its logic, and its ignoring of any notion of an afterlife must have smacked of *kufr* (unbelief) to him, a charge that the level-headed al-Wahidi defended the poet against. The second example, from a poem honoring the secretary, Abu ʿAli Harun ibn ʿAbd al-ʿAziz al-Awraji, who was a follower of a Sufi order, shares the same attention to logic, leading to a paradoxical conclusion – something often disapproved by Arab critics – but with no immediate theological implication:

> You have shown generosity to the point that it almost turned to avarice because of its great extent, [just as] there is weeping that comes from happiness.
>
> (W., 200)

Similarly, al-Sahib ibn ʿAbbad and others found fault with al-Mutanabbi for using the "difficult language and ambiguous conceits" of the Sufis in verses such as:

> If it weren't that I am not asleep
> I would have thought I was a specter of myself.
>
> (W., 217)

The critical bristling at al-Mutanabbi's dependence on conceits derived from the twists of logic – sometimes, but certainly not always, with theologically challenging results – specifically evokes the debate of roughly a century earlier over the poetry of al-Mutanabbi's predecessor, Abu Tammam. Like al-Mutanabbi, Abu Tammam was attacked for too freely indulging in the type of philosophizing that dominated Arab intellectual circles in the ninth century. This, the critics charged, often resulted in convoluted expression, which they contrasted with the supposedly fluid and unforced expression of Abu Tammam's younger colleague, al-Buhturi (d. 897 CE), that many saw as the Bedouin legacy of Arabic poetry.

In contrast, the poetic expression of universal truths and aphorisms scattered throughout al-Mutanabbi's verse was frequently praised. Al-Tha'alibi's positive treatment of al-Mutanabbi's aphorisms, although little more than a catalogue of exemplary verses and half-lines, is the longest section in his chapter on the poet. Al-Qadi al-Jurjani also praised al-Mutanabbi's proverb-making. Even Abu 'Ali al-Hatimi (d. 998 CE), al-Mutanabbi's Baghdad nemesis, produced a short treatise containing some ninety-three parallels between al-Mutanabbi's verse and pseudo-Aristotelian wisdoms (Bonebakker, 34). The approving tone of the author is striking, given the derisively critical tenor of the author's other works on al-Mutanabbi. Indeed, the title of al-Hatimi's longer treatise about the debate(s) that he claimed took place between him and al-Mutanabbi contains a revealing double entendre, and can be read as either *The Clarifying Treatise Concerning the Plagiarisms of Abu'l-Tayyib al-Mutanabbi and the Inferior among His Poetry* or *The Lacerating Treatise Concerning ...* This work, which describes four debates between al-Hatimi and al-Mutanabbi, the first at the poet's residence and the subsequent three at the house of the Buyid vizier, al-Muhallabi, presents al-Mutanabbi as a mediocre pretender, guilty of plagiarism as well as poor style.

Much about the treatise's renditions of these debates seems implausible. The three meetings in al-Muhallabi's house probably never took place, for, as Bonebakker has pointed out, it is unlikely "that Mutanabbi should have allowed himself to be publicly humiliated on four different occasions" (52). At one point al-Mutanabbi is castigated for pretending not to be familiar with the poetry of Abu Tammam and al-Buhturi, which seems unbelievable. Throughout the text, the poet comes across as a "straight man" who is given the floor only for brief statements that set the stage for his opponents to make points in the debate. Bonebakker's careful analysis of the various versions of the debate concludes that the long *Clarifying Treatise* is merely an extended version of the shorter versions that recount only the first meeting between al-Mutanabbi and al-Hatimi in front of the poet's students (51), and that both Mu'izz al-Dawlah and al-Muhallabi had nothing to do with the dispute between al-Hatimi and al-Mutanabbi and "were only introduced later by Hatimi to enhance his own prestige" (35). Al-Hatimi's favorable treatment of al-Mutanabbi's aphorisms in the shorter work just mentioned constitutes the positive presentation of the poet promised at the end of the short version of the first debate between the two men.

THE LIMITS OF IMAGINATION

Many of the poets and critics who wrote about al-Mutanabbi's poetry spoke admiringly of the novelty of some of his conceits and topics. Al-Qadi al-Jurjani praised al-Mutanabbi's poem describing a severe fever that befell him, which he deemed original and the product of both astute craft and natural talent. The poet al-Sariy al-Raffa', on at least one occasion, praised al-Mutanabbi, saying, "By God, that is a conceit that the ancients could not have come up with." Al-Mutanabbi's rival, al-Nami, likewise acknowledged two conceits he said no one had ever used and that he wished he could have thought of before al-Mutanabbi.

None the less, many of al-Mutanabbi's individual conceits were criticized. Some the critics deemed far-fetched, such as in the verse in al-Mutanabbi's elegy on Sayf al-Dawlah's sister, Khawlah:

> The part of her hair causes happiness in the hearts of perfume
> and regret in the hearts of helmets and leather shields.

(W., 609)

Others were considered overly complicated, requiring too much thought. The traditional expectation that a verse's meaning should reach the mind as soon as its sound hit the ear prevailed.

Perhaps the most persistent criticism of the poet's conceits was that he sometimes went too far in his use of exaggeration – a subject much debated in critical circles up to and beyond the time of al-Mutanabbi. So prominent was hyperbole in the work of al-Mutanabbi that the eleventh-century critic, Ibn Rashiq al-Qayrawani, in his *The Foundation Regarding the Beauties of Poetry and Its Norms and Its Criticism*, viewed it, disapprovingly, as the mainstay of his entire style. It is clear from the examples he cites, and from his own words, that it is specifically the irreverence entailed in al-Mutanabbi's hyperbole that Ibn Rashiq finds troubling. For example, in an amatory verse composed in his youth, al-Mutanabbi's use of the word *tawhid*, which refers to the profession of faith in the oneness of God that is the core Muslim belief, was clearly provocative. Al-Tha'alibi states directly that this is one of a number of verses that indicate "weak religious belief." While he acknowledges that "religion is no measure of a poet's rank, nor is inferior faith reason to assign a poet a lesser rank, Islam is still due a certain reverence that should not be violated in word or action, poetry or prose" (*The Matchless Pearl*, 184):

> They suck drops of saliva from my mouth,
> sweeter there than the declaration of faith.

(W., 30)

The critics specifically rejected the use of hyperbole in that it led to conceits based on the impossible or the nonexistent – in other words, the fantastic. They generally did not like the components of metaphors to stray too far from their ontological moorings, thus denying the limits of reality. Not until the brilliant literary theorist, 'Abd al-Qahir al-Jurjani (d. 1078 or 1081), discussed the fantastic in a manner that retained its palatability from a theological point of view did Arabic criticism find a way to accommodate hyperbole and paradox somewhat more comfortably. By the time of al-Mutanabbi, the demand for description faithful to reality which often fettered the imaginative production of earlier poets was somewhat less, but it was not yet possible for our poet to totally escape critical disapproval.

BORROWING VERSUS PLAGIARISM

One obsessive focus in the vast body of criticism of al-Mutanabbi's verse was on the notion of *sariqa*, literally "theft." Many works were written pointing out all the verses that al-Mutanabbi had plagiarized from earlier poets, both "ancients" and "moderns." This issue was the source of much debate, however, due to the lack of agreement about where the line could be drawn between legitimate borrowing and unacceptable plagiarism. The reason for the ambiguity was that, as pointed out earlier, Arabic poetry was a public event. The long-established practice of producing *mu'arada*s or *contrefacta* of well-known poems (in which a later poet composed a piece using the same meter and rhyme as a poem by a well-known predecessor, perhaps also mimicking some of his diction, either to pay homage to or outdo the work of the earlier poet), conveys the communal nature of the poetic experience for Arab practitioners and aficionados. By al-Mutanabbi's time poetry was often first recorded in writing, but it was still meant to be recited publicly and appreciated by a listening audience. Poets were expected to insert key words or even entire verses of earlier poets into their verse, and the audience's recognition of these components constituted part of their shared enjoyment.

The 'Abbasid poets, whose poetry was increasingly manneristic, were particularly expected to make reference to the highly esteemed poetry of the "ancients" and even the acknowledged greats among their predecessors in the "modern" period. Originality was expected, but its relationship to the inherited body of poetic production had to be identifiable. In this poetic environment, it was often difficult to define originality and to draw the line between acceptable allusion to or manipulation of a predecessor's idea and outright theft.

Theorists composed lists of the various types of poetic borrowing that could occur, but there was little agreement about the definitions or even the nomenclature. Ibn Waki' made a valiant attempt to delineate a system for identifying and evaluating poetic borrowing, indicating admirable and blameworthy types in his presentation. When it came to evaluating the work of al-Mutanabbi on the basis of his own system, however, Ibn Waki' differed little either from his predecessors in the field of literary theory, or from his contemporaries concerned exclusively with al-Mutanabbi's borrowings, and often provided lengthy poetic genealogies of individual verses. In one instance, a verse by al-Mutanabbi from a poem in praise of al-Husayn ibn Ishaq al-Tanukhi was criticized by al-Hatimi as having been taken from a line by Bashshar ibn Burd. Al-Mutanabbi's verse is:

[He is] a young man, like black clouds, both feared and hoped for
The rain from them is wished for, while their thunderbolts are feared.

(W., 124)

Bashshar's verse is:

People hope for and fear your two states,
as if you were [both] paradise and hellfire.

Ibn Waki' cites a verse al-Mutanabbi's commentators attribute to Abu Tammam which, although it is not in his *diwan*, is much closer to al-Mutanabbi's:

Liberality and might in thunderbolts and rain
when they come together in a collection of overhanging clouds

Not content, Ibn Waki' goes on to name four other poets from whom this poetic idea is supposedly taken, stating that "both the construction and ideas of these verses are similar."

From this example, it is clear that the notion of borrowing covered an expansive territory: for al-Hatimi the simple sharing of the same basic idea was enough to claim borrowing, while for Ibn Waki' a more specific overlap was needed. Many of al-Mutanabbi's critics, such as al-Hatimi, were interested in little more than discrediting the poet by denying him any precedence based on a claim of originality. Competition among poets, critics, and connoisseurs — even ones on the same side of the argument – to find precedent verses was the rule of the day.

Ibn Jinni tells the story of al-Mutanabbi boasting that Ibn Hinzaba, one of Kafur's viziers in Egypt, told him: "Did you know that I brought together all my books and a group of literary experts to search out for me where you took this conceit from and they were unable to do so?" And al-Mutanabbi noted: "He had more books than anyone I've ever seen." Ibn Jinni goes on to boast that he had found the same idea, expressed as elegantly as in al-Mutanabbi's verse, in a hemistich by Ibn al-Mu'tazz. (*al-Subh al-munabbi*, 288) The problem with the treatment of borrowing in al-Mutanabbi's poetry is that there is very little discussion of the contexts in which the various verses occurred and the role they played in the complete poems. Not until the work of 'Abd al-Qahir al-Jurjani was there any rigorous understanding of the issues underlying the question of poetic borrowing. 'Abd al-Qahir differentiated between a general idea shared by the community at large – which by its very nature was not susceptible to theft – and a particular formulation or uniquely worded version of it, and also provided, through his concept of *sura* (form), the basis for evaluating the role of a unit of discourse within a textual whole.

SUMMING UP

Despite the undeniable nit-picking among critics of al-Mutanabbi's poetry, there is a consistent, if sometimes reluctant, recognition of his overall excellence as a poet. Even one of his fiercest critics, al-Sahib ibn 'Abbad, shows his grudging appreciation in his numerous citations of the poet's verse in his own writing.

Al-Mutanabbi's claims of greatness, coupled with the measureless worship of his cult of admirers, seems to have engendered much of the critical debate over his poetry. Theoretically, there was little new in this body of criticism. More lamentably, there was sparse appreciation of the elements that made al-Mutanabbi's poetry stand out. At times, the critics put their finger on important features of the poetry but failed to appreciate their significance. When, for example, al-Wahidi notices al-Mutanabbi's tendency to present himself as sharing the qualities of his patron, he merely wonders why the poet's patrons would tolerate such insolence.

There were exceptions; writers such as al-Tha'alibi zeroed in on some of the saliently new aspects of al-Mutanabbi's style. In particular he admired al-Mutanabbi's habit of addressing his patrons in a manner that would normally be used for a lover or friend, rather than a ruler. Al-Tha'alibi was also complimentary of al-Mutanabbi's use of terms from love poetry to describe war and other serious topics. Unfortunately, in neither case does the critic provide any discussion of the implications of the features he so astutely singled out.

This is not to say that these aficionados of poetry did not have a sense of the overall effect of these and other techniques used by al-Mutanabbi. On the contrary, so little analytical discussion was presented partly because so much could be assumed to be understood by an expert audience. The fact that features such as those pinpointed by al-Tha'alibi are intimately related to the organizing principles of al-Mutanabbi's poetry went unremarked.

The terms of the critical debate about al-Mutanabbi hardly differed from those of the debate over the poetry of Abu Tammam a century earlier. Like his predecessor, al-Mutanabbi was accused of writing as a philosopher rather than a poet, but while Abu Tammam became the poster-boy for convoluted expression and recondite reasoning, al-Mutanabbi's popular touch, shown in his ability to give proverbial truths an elegant poetic turn, spared him a measure of opprobrium on this count. But where Abu Tammam was judged primarily against the model of the pre-Islamic and early Islamic poets, al-Mutanabbi was compared also to the now recognized "modern" masters, Abu Tammam and al-Buhturi, from whom he was accused of borrowing freely.

The poet's legacy was assured. While in the century after al-Mutanabbi's death his followers concentrated more on the oral transmission of the poet's *diwan* than on written critical treatises about his work, some composed responses to their master's harshest critics. Ibn Jinni (d. 1002 CE), the close protégé of the man he referred to as "our poet," was diligent in this regard. His three works on al-Mutanabbi's poetry included, in addition to a large and a smaller commentary on the *diwan*, a rebuttal of Ibn Waki' that is now lost. Ibn Jinni's work was philological, complete with the same competitive hair-splitting and one-upmanship that characterized other treatises on al-Mutanabbi. In some of the numerous treatises that were composed to rebut Ibn Jinni, he was openly mocked as one who knew nothing about literary criticism, which he should best leave to the experts.

Thanks to the dedicatedly nurtured lines of transmission and study extending out across the Islamic lands from Baghdad and Egypt to generations of important commentators and scholars, such as the poet, al-Ma'arri (d. 1058 CE), and the famed prose writer, al-Tawhidi (d. 1023 CE), al-Mutanabbi's poetry became dominant up to and throughout the so-called "age of stagnation" in post-classical (thirteenth- to eighteenth-century) Arabic poetry. We can only guess at the importance of more informal transmission on the part of the middle-class consumers who frequented the al-Basri circle in Baghdad and their associates.

If al-Mutanabbi's contemporaries failed to uncover what was truly innovative in his poetry, modern Arab critics, despite their often unrestrained admiration of the poet, offered little more. It was the practitioners themselves, rather than the critics, who truly understood and built on the innovations of al-Mutanabbi's style. In the following chapter we will examine how later poets were influenced by al-Mutanabbi and take a look at some of the ways they resisted, co-opted, and imitated al-Mutanabbi's verse. Just as al-Mutanabbi stood, whether he admitted it or not, on the shoulders of his predecessors, so too did generations of later poets build on the rich poetic legacy of our poet.

6

THE HIGHEST FORM OF PRAISE

Perhaps the most eloquent testimony to the importance of al-Mutanabbi's poetry is the profound and centuries-long influence it has exerted over poets writing in Arabic, Persian, and Hebrew. Al-Mutanabbi's work was extensively studied and transmitted in Persia and became part and parcel of the cultural legacy of poets educated in both the Arabic and Persian literary traditions.

In the thirteenth century, as the caliphate of Baghdad was falling to the invading Mongols, the renowned Persian poet from Shiraz, Saʻdi (d. 1292 CE), was making use of many of the themes and motifs found in al-Mutanabbi's *oeuvre*. The influence of al-Mutanabbi's poetry on Saʻdi has been amply documented. Saʻdi's emphasis, in his most famous works, on the treachery of fate and the perfidy of enemies, coupled with his deft formulation of aphorisms, has a clear Mutanabbian ring. As with al-Mutanabbi, it is partly because of the compelling commonsense appeal of his proverbial exhortations that much of his verse has become part of common parlance in Persian. Despite his general tone of tolerance and goodwill, Saʻdi also shared some of al-Mutanabbi's less attractive predilections, including an antipathy toward black people and sometimes women.

The influence of Arabic poetry on pre-modern Hebrew verse in the context of the cultural melting-pot of Islamic Spain has been even more widely recognized. Poets such as the Toledo-born Judah ha-Levi (d. 1142 CE) employed not only the classical Arabic poetic meters, and the non-canonical verse forms then in vogue in Andalusia, but also many of the poetic modes and motifs that dominated in Arabic verse. The outstanding 'Abbasid poets, such as Abu Tammam and al-Buhturi, as well as al-Mutanabbi, were studied and emulated. Numerous precise parallels between conceits in ha-Levi's and al-Mutanabbi's verse can be cited as evidence of our poet's specific influence.

The most profound echo of al-Mutanabbi can be found in poetry composed in Arabic from the mid tenth century up until today. It is hard to identify another Arab poet who has exerted so far-reaching and so continuous an influence over the development of Arabic poetry in its diverse environments and forms.

ANDALUSIAN ADMIRER

Al-Mutanabbi's grand style and heroic value system resonated with his Andalusian contemporary, Ibn Hani' (ca. 934/938–973 CE), a dedicated Isma'ili Shi'ite whose undisguised beliefs eventually forced his departure from Muslim Spain. In his new North African home, Ibn Hani' became the court poet of the fourth Fatimid caliph, al-Mu'izz li-Din Allah, for whom his panegyrics constituted a propaganda tool that found an audience in both east and west. In 969, when al-Mu'izz's general, Jawhar, conquered Egypt, Ibn Hani' composed a congratulatory panegyric for his patron that was an imitation of a poem composed by al-Mutanabbi in honor of 'Ali ibn Ahmad 'Amir al-Antaki. Like other *contrefacta*, Ibn Hani's poem used the same rhyme and meter as the model, but was sixty lines longer than the forty-one-verse original. Dubbed by many the "Mutanabbi of the west," Ibn Hani' applied al-Mutanabbi's grand rhetorical style and exalted ideals not merely to celebrate the Fatimid conquest of Egypt, but especially to interpret it from within the framework of Isma'ili sectarian beliefs. Ibn Hani' represents Jawhar's success over Egypt as the victory of the legitimate rulers of the Muslim community over the usurper 'Abbasids and the re-establishment of the heirs of 'Ali. Employing a phrase used in verse 44 of chapter 11 ("Hud") of the Qur'an, in the context of the description of the end of the flood, the first verse declares: "The family of al-'Abbas says: 'Has Egypt been conquered?'/Say to the 'Abbasids: 'The matter has been settled.'" The ascendance of the Fatimids is characterized as a monumental event in human history, divinely decreed and providentially directed. The 'Abbasids are exhorted to leave the people to their rightful rulers, the Fatimids, for they have no claim to leadership authority (v. 20). Not only is al-Mu'izz called the "imam," whom the populace is called upon to obey (v. 13), but in several, plainly blasphemous, verses he is likened first to a prophet, then to God:

> I consider praising him to be like praising God:
> it is serving God and glorifying his name, which lessen the burden of sin.
>
> (*Diwan*, 139)

Like Jesus, whose prophethood, according to the Qur'an, was clear even in the cradle, the marks of al-Mu'izz's special role in Islam were apparent to his father even when he was an infant (v. 48).

Why did Ibn Hani' choose the particular poem by al-Mutanabbi that he did, on which to pattern his own piece, and what does the dialogue with the earlier poem contribute? The poem by al-Mutanabbi is not one to Sayf al-Dawlah, Kafur, or any of the more significant patrons for whom the poet wrote. On the contrary, it was dedicated to a man who was a chancellery official in the Ikhshidid government that held sway in Syria at a time when the poet, lacking more appealing sponsorship, resorted to trying to curry the favor of that administration.

The poem is as much boast as praise. Al-Mutanabbi's poem presents a portrait of an heroic ideal not entirely co-opted by the exigencies of political attachment or official patronage. It is that heroic ideal that al-Mu'izz is depicted as fulfilling – and indeed surpassing – as he is presented by Ibn Hani' as the one true caliph and imam. Ibn Hani's is not a poem of perfunctory praise to an indifferent political figure who might serve as a source of bounty, but rather a paean to someone who fulfills a unique religious and political role in the poet's Shi'ite world-view. By engaging al-Mutanabbi's poem, Ibn Hani' redefines his own role as praise poet and propagandist while identifying with the heroic ideal and rhetorical grandeur of his predecessor's work.

KINDRED SPIRITS

Ironically, a student of the companions of al-Mutanabbi's old nemesis, Ibn Khalawayh, the poet and prose writer Abu'l 'Ala' al-Ma'arri (973–1058 CE), was to become perhaps the most fanatical of all admirers of al-Mutanabbi's poetry. Known for referring to al-Mutanabbi not by name, but rather as "the poet," al-Ma'arri shared his predecessor's extravagant pride and critical nature, and especially his idiosyncratic views on religion.

Al-Ma'arri was a student of Muhammad ibn 'Abd Allah ibn Sa'd, who was a transmitter of al-Mutanabbi's poetry. His zeal for the poet may even have gotten him into some trouble in Baghdad. When al-Murtada, the brother of the Shi'ite poet, al-Sharif al-Radi, found fault with al-Mutanabbi's verse, al-Ma'arri publicly criticized him. Subsequently, when al-Ma'arri attended al-Murtada's literary salon, his host had him dragged out by the feet. Blind from the age of four, al-Ma'arri exhibited a fierce spiritual and intellectual independence throughout his life. These boastful verses from his first *diwan* of poetry are strongly reminiscent of al-Mutanabbi's prideful declarations and unfettered conceit:

> My reputation has spread through the land, so who among them can
> extinguish a sun whose light is everywhere
> The nights would be burdened by
> even a part of what I carry in my heart
> And Mount Radwa would be weighed down
> by less than I bear
> Although I came late, I will
> achieve what the ancients could not
> I go forth in the morning, though the morning

be sharp swords
and travel by night, though the
darkness be mighty armies.

(*Saqt al-zand*, 42–43)

Likewise, al-Maʿarri's notorious pessimism, so like the sentiment al-Mutanabbi sometimes expressed, is conveyed in these verses, which are well known to generations of Arabs from all walks of life:

Walk gently about in the air, if you can
not strutting over the remains of other men
Many a tomb has become tomb again and again
amused at the pressing together of adversaries
and of one corpse against the remains of another
over the length of endless ages.

(*Saqt al-zand*, 82)

Al-Maʿarri also produced a full commentary on al-Mutanabbi's poetry, *Muʿjiz Ahmad*, which was edited in 1988. By referring to the Muslim belief in prophetic miracles, the title of this work – *Ahmad's Miracle* – plays on the poet's sobriquet, "al-Mutanabbi," meaning "the would-be prophet."

Much as al-Maʿarri admired al-Mutanabbi and sought to emulate him in his poetry, rarely did he produce anything more sustained than a fleeting echo of the poet's style and tone. His verse lacked al-Mutanabbi's consistent manipulation of the individual persona and his personal experience as an organizing principle, which often provided a rhetorical as well as psychological unity for al-Mutanabbi's poems. True awareness of this most salient feature of al-Mutanabbi's poetry, and the ability to emulate it, would be left to much later generations of poets.

THE CLASSICAL AS INNOVATION

In his 1928 work, *The History of Arabic Literature*, Ahmad al-Zayyat commented that al-Mutanabbi was "the leader of the romantic school in Arabic poetry" (227; Blachère, 307). Since the romantic movement did not make itself felt until the early 1930s, this remark was provocative indeed.

It is certainly true that for the neoclassical poets writing at the end of the nineteenth and the beginning of the twentieth century, the 'Abbasid greats, including al-Mutanabbi, Abu Tammam, al-Buhturi, and Abu Nuwas, ushered Arabic poetry into a new, more dynamic era of literary creation generally known as the Arabic literary "renaissance." It was partly through numerous *contrefacta* of poems from the 'Abbasid period that early modern Arabic poets dug their way out of the relative doldrums that Arabic poetry had languished in for several centuries, to produce a poetry that was more relevant to the immediate circumstances of the world they lived in.

One of the earliest pioneers of neoclassical poetry, Mahmud Sami al-Barudi (1839–1904), produced numerous imitations of al-Mutanabbi's poems, including a boast ("I accepted from the world that which I did not want …") in which he complains of the despotic government then in power in Egypt. Though the relevant khedive is not named, he may easily have been referring to the latter days of Isma'il's rule (1863–1879) or to his successor, Tawfiq (1879–1892).

The poem uses the same meter and rhyme letter as al-Mutanabbi's poem ("I wanted from the days that which they do not like …"), which is one of his early panegyrics to Kafur, composed in 957 when the poet still hoped for a governorship from the Ikhshidid regent. In addition to using some of its phrasing and diction, al-Barudi's poem includes direct citation of signature half-lines from the original work and rephrasings of ideas contained in other poems by al-Mutanabbi. In particular, after a long amatory prelude/complaint in which al-Barudi laments the impossibility of love or true friendship, the pernicious effect of infatuation on reasonable men, and the perfidy of time, which turns his hair white, the poet quotes as the second half of his verse 31 the first hemistich of al-Mutanabbi's first line: "I wanted from the days that which they do not like." Only then does the poet suggest what the focus of his attention and concern is, as he alludes to his disillusionment with the political authorities by whom he had once been favored:

> If I have abandoned contentment, it is only after having
> kept company with an age whose slave angers the free man.
>
> (*Diwan*, 1:192)

Throughout the poem al-Barudi produces gnomic lines after the fashion of al-Mutanabbi, in particular presenting in the second hemistich of a given line an aphorism that explains and universalizes the sentiment expressed in the first half, as al-Mutanabbi often did. The very first line is typical:

> I accepted from the world that which I did not want
> And what man's forearm is the equal of fate?
>
> (*Diwan*, 1:187)

As with al-Mutanabbi's poetry, this mechanism must have played a significant role in the "marketing" of al-Barudi's poetry. Neoclassical poetry at the dawn of the modern era was very much the poetry of an elite, but gradually, with the spread of education and political engagement, poets like al-Barudi and his successors began to reach a wider audience. Aphorisms, in their economic expression of universal truths recognizable by all, made a didactic, declamatory style of poetry somewhat more accessible to a diverse audience.

In the second half of his poem, without making specific reference to the object of his or his listeners' resentment, al-Barudi concentrates on a vigorous call to resistance to oppression cast in terms borrowed from classical Arabic poetic conceits. Numerous verses are specific echoes of al-Mutanabbi lines:

> Whoever is debased because of fear of death, his life is
> more injurious to him than any death that may befall him
> The most lethal of maladies is the eye seeing a tyrant
> doing harm while his praises are sung in assemblies.
>
> (*Diwan*, 1:192)

Al-Barudi was known as "master of the sword and the pen" and was a high-ranking army officer, eventually imprisoned and exiled for his leadership of the 'Urabi revolt in 1882. Because of his military experience and reputation, his verses are enlivened beyond the confines of their conventional poetic origins:

> Until when will we wander at night in the darkness of trials
> in which the scabbard is too tight to hold the sword?
>
> If a man does not push back the hand of oppression when it strikes
> then he cannot regret when his honor is lost
>
> It is a shame for a man to accept debasement
> when the sword is sufficient to right the matter.
>
> (*Diwan*, 1: 192–193)

What qualities does al-Barudi's evocation of his predecessor's poem lend to his work? What is the artistic effect of this inter-textual dialogue? It is clear that al-Barudi wishes to summon up the classical Arab heroic values in an effort to raise the consciousness of his listeners and rouse them to action. More subtly, he is evoking the shame and disappointment endured by al-Mutanabbi at the hands of Kafur. Unlike al-Mutanabbi when he composed the original poem, al-Barudi and his audience know the outcome of the poet's pleas and valiant effort to rationalize his association with the regent. For the nineteenth-century al-Barudi and the consumers of his poetry, al-Mutanabbi's shame is as iconic as his ethnic pride and his adherence to a heroic self-image. By alluding to it indirectly in his poem, al-Barudi is implicitly warning his audience of the dire results their own inaction could have. Al-Mutanabbi thus serves not only as the revered mouthpiece of traditional values and Arab pride, but also as a cautionary case study for his listeners' edification, as they are urged by the poet to take action and not be duped by dishonest rulers.

For al-Barudi and the neoclassical poets, evoking the classical Arabic poetic tradition was an act of identification and empowerment. By demonstrating mastery of the traditional poetic forms and diction, the neoclassical poets claimed a status equal to that of their 'Abbasid predecessors and the authority to edify and shape public opinion that it implied. For al-Barudi, who was known for his pride and willingness to declare his own superiority, the identification with al-Mutanabbi must have been much deeper and more personal. As with many inter-textual encounters, there is a competitive undertone to this pairing of poems, as al-Barudi invites his listeners to succeed where al-Mutanabbi failed.

NEOCLASSICAL VOICE

Al-Mutanabbi was a personal favorite not only of al-Barudi, but also of the "prince of poets," Ahmad Shawqi (1868–1932), probably the best-known and most influential of the neoclassical poets.

In some of Shawqi's *contrefacta* it is the personal voice of al-Mutanabbi of all the aspects of his poetry that is most fully engaged. One such is Ahmad Shawqi's elegy on his own mother, composed while in exile in Spain, which is an echo of al-Mutanabbi's elegy on his grandmother. There is a notable difference between the two works, for where al-Mutanabbi's sadness is given shape by his compulsion to assert responsibility even in the face of events over which he has no control, Shawqi emphasizes his victimhood. His grief over the loss of his mother is conflated with the sadness of exile and sadness over the orphanhood of others resulting from the recent war, and he emphasizes his lack of culpability in this indivisible constellation of tragedies. By summoning up his predecessor's poem, Shawqi creates a shared poetic terrain with al-Mutanabbi, associating himself with his artistic grandeur and status. He is borrowing the unified personal voice and existential rehabilitation that his 'Abbasid predecessor offers in his composition. As with al-Barudi's poem, Shawqi's elegy is what it is because it exists in dialogue with al-Mutanabbi's poem. Without this dialogue, the personal power that al-Mutanabbi strives for in his poem is lacking in Shawqi's elegy:

> I swear by the care you lent me in infancy
> And your having rendered my body the greatest act of kindness

And by a grave hung with majesty
Adorned with time honored attributes in abundance and new virtues aplenty
That I had no opinion or leaning regarding the war
And I did not want this bereavement and orphanhood for people.

(Diwan, 2:535)

MODERN ECHOES

Ahmad al-Zayyat was not alone in recognizing the modernist spirit of al-Mutanabbi's poetry. The famous Palestinian poet, Mahmud Darwish (1941–), recently roused the ire of many of his fellow poets by suggesting that al-Mutanabbi was the most modern of Arab poets: "When we search for a diagnosis of our current situation, we resort to citing excerpts from the poetry of al-Mutanabbi, which makes me feel that this great poet remains more lively and modern and contemporary than we are" (*Al- Jadid*, vol. 2, nos. 50/51, 2005, 15). In the storm that followed this and other comments in the same vein, none of Darwish's critics, despite their embarrassment and eagerness to redeem their generation, dissented from his evaluation of al-Mutanabbi as a poet.

The frequency with which al-Mutanabbi appears, as icon, muse, or mask, in the poetry of modern Arab poets is striking. In Nasir-controlled 1960s Egypt, artists, especially those critical of government policies, constantly sought ways to express their views without exposing themselves to censorship and official retribution. During this era, allegory and symbolism took on new importance in Arabic literature, both prose and poetry.

The Egyptian poet, Amal Dunqul (1940–1983), in his poem *From al-Mutanabbi's Memoirs (in Egypt)*, spoke with the voice of his famed poet ancestor to present a critique of those in power. The poem was written on the first anniversary of the Egyptian defeat in the 1967 Six-Day War with Israel. It opens with the poet's declaration that despite his natural dislike of alcohol, he has become used to it since becoming a "parrot" in the court of Fustat. The regent Kafur is represented in the same derogatory terms that al-Mutanabbi used for him, with references to his "pierced lip, black face, and plundered manhood." As al-Mutanabbi did, Dunqul bemoans the fate of Arabness, which has none but this inadequate protector, Kafur, and complains of having to praise his valiant sword while it is actually in its sheath, being eaten away by rust. He recalls Khawlah, the sister of Sayf al-Dawlah, who, despite her valor in battle against the Byzantines, was ultimately taken prisoner. Unaided by the citizens, she remains in Byzantine captivity, calling out to Kafur for aid. When told, Kafur orders his servant to buy a Byzantine slave-girl and flog her so that she will call out miserably for Byzantine aid, "so that there will be an eye for an eye and a tooth for a tooth." The poet thus implicitly mocks the empty bravado of the Egyptian ruler. Next, the poet summons up the image of Sayf al-Dawlah, who, in contrast to the anti-hero Kafur, valiantly battles the Byzantine enemy, to whom he leaves "nothing but blood and tears." Upon his return from battle, exhausted but smiling, the small children of Aleppo call out to him: "Oh, savior of the Arabs." When Kafur falls asleep and the court relaxes, the poet's slave-girl requests that he hire guards to protect their house, "for the thieves have gotten out of hand in Egypt." The tone of mockery conveyed by the sing-song quality of the verses that constitute his response culminates with the clear indictment: "What need do I have of a drawn sword as long as I am under the protection of Kafur?" Dunqul closes the poem with a rewriting of the ode composed by al-Mutanabbi on the eve of the Feast of the Sacrifice in January, 962, the day before he fled Egypt ("Feast day, in what state do you return …"). This pastiche ends with a direct call to action to the people of Egypt:

> I called out: Must the waters flow with blood
> in order for you to overflow and people awaken when they are summoned?
> Feast day, in what state do you return, oh feast?

It is clear that his intention is to liken the Egyptian president, Gamal 'Abd al-Nasir, to the eunuch Kafur. As provocative as this poem is, such bold criticism would have been inconceivable without the voice of al-Mutanabbi to hide behind. Obsessed, like Dunqul, with the idea of Arab ascendancy and might, and yearning like him for effective Arab leadership, al-Mutanabbi represented the perfect vehicle for the Egyptian poet's indictment of Nasir's regime.

The extent to which modern Arab poets view al-Mutanabbi's history as relevant to the events of today is clear from a poem composed in the 1980s by Mahmud Darwish: *Al-Mutanabbi's Voyage to Egypt*. In this piece, the poet takes on the voice of his tenth-century predecessor to comment on his disappointment, both personal and political, with Egypt, the site of al-Mutanabbi's frustrating experience at the hands of the Ikhshidid regent, Kafur. The sense of alienation and sadness at the loss of his homeland is underlined by the contrast between Aleppo, Iraq, and "the North," on the one hand, and Egypt on the other. The journey, referred to by the Arabic word, *rahil*, which also connotes the passage section of the classical Arabic ode, is presented as an existential search for the ideal of a homeland and for an individual wholeness and sense of self. Egypt provides neither:

> My nation is my new ode
> I walk toward my self and it drives me from Fustat
> How often I enter mirrors
> How often I shatter them
> and they shatter me

In the voice of the 'Abbasid poet who longed for a political appointment from the manipulative Kafur, the modern Palestinian poet, who has witnessed the formation of the state of Israel in his homeland, complains of seeing "nations handed out like gifts." Addressing Egypt, bound by the Camp David accords to *détente* with its former enemy, he says: "Whenever I tried to cry with your eyes, you turned to my enemy." Like al-Mutanabbi, he laments the spread of Byzantines around Arabs with "no sword or arm to chase them." Finally, with the resuscitated pride and power of al-Mutanabbi departing from Kafur's Fustat, he declares:

> I am the Qarmatian – I would sell the palace for a song
> and destroy it with a song
> I lean my frame against the wind and my wounded spirit
> I cannot be bought.

Al-Mutanabbi's bitter experience with Kafur, who is called "the deceiver" in this poem, becomes the vehicle for expressing frustration with modern Egypt's failure to stand up for Arab pride and Palestinian sovereignty. Just as al-Mutanabbi's self-respect caused him eventually to abandon the Egyptian capital, so too the poetic persona's soul drives him from Fustat. He chooses to be true to himself and remain an upstart "Qarmatian" who resists the oppression of the "slave prince," Egypt. In al-Mutanabbi, Darwish saw a unique combination of political longing and personal angst that coincided with his experience as a modern Palestinian poet, struggling similarly for reconciliation of his political ambitions and his identity as a poet.

In contrast, the Iraqi poet, 'Abd al-Wahhab al-Bayyati (1926–1999), summons up the figure of al-Mutanabbi and details of his professional life in a poem from 1964, *The Death of al-Mutanabbi*, as an attempt to redefine the role of the poet and of poetry in society. A life-long Marxist, al-Bayyati rejects the notion of political control over poetry, represented by al-Mutanabbi's jobs as panegyrist to corrupt and abusive rulers. Borrowing from a phrase in one of al-Mutanabbi's poems, he claims: "Rabbits, that's what kings are," and insists that the role of poetry is to be the voice of the underrepresented in society and the vehicle for change:

> Tear up the poet and the dinar
> And let the caliph eat the leaves and dust
> And let poetry
> be saved

Having, over the course of this multi-voiced piece, reconstituted al-Mutanabbi in keeping with his Marxist philosophy, al-Bayyati ends with the acknowledgement that al-Mutanabbi "hovers on the walls of Baghdad and in her market places."

Numerous other modern Arab poets, including 'Umar Abu Rishah, Khalil Hawi, al-Akhtal al-Saghir, and al-Jawahiri, have made use of the poetry and the image of al-Mutanabbi. Most notable is 'Ali Ahmad Sa'id, known as Adunis (1930–), who produced a complex three-volume work, *The Book. The Place's Yesterday Now: A Manuscript Attributed to al-Mutanabbi*, which is a multi-voiced treatment of Arab and Islamic history and a meditation on the function of poetry and the role of the poet in society. This work, which bears such eloquent testimony to the influence of al-Mutanabbi on modern Arab poets, sorely deserves an in-depth study – something that is beyond the scope of this book.

CONCLUSION

We have examined the salient features of al-Mutanabbi's poetry that have guaranteed it the important place in Arab culture it has enjoyed since the tenth century. Al-Mutanabbi's mastery of the classical and contemporary poetic tradition, from the pre-Islamic poets to the "moderns" of the 'Abbasid period, is a main ingredient that explains his wide-reaching appeal.

The extent to which he had absorbed the poetry of his predecessors partly accounts for the persistent charges of plagiarism that were leveled against him by contemporary critics. Master of the grand style, al-Mutanabbi made his verse accessible to a broader range of people through his wielding of aphorism and the inescapable wisdom it encompasses. This common – or, at least, universal – touch, along with al-Mutanabbi's attentive cultivation of his *diwan* and its transmission, has put the poet's verse on the lips of people from diverse social and educational backgrounds throughout the centuries. Al-Mutanabbi's verse has become so ingrained in the Arab cultural fabric that it is not uncommon to hear even illiterate people quote verses they have heard and memorized for their proverbial wisdom. Verses such as "If you hear an inferior blaming me/it is evidence that I am superior" (W., 265) and "If you honor one who is noble, you become his master/but if you honor one who is base, he will become rebellious" (W., 529) are widely employed in everyday social intercourse wherever Arabic is spoken. Furthermore, the poet's artful attention to the musicality of his verses facilitated memorization and guaranteed their repetition.

It might reasonably be argued that much of what I have talked about can also be found in the poetry of the other masters of the 'Abbasid era, such as Abu Tammam, al-Buhturi, Abu Nuwas, and Ibn al-Rumi. They too mastered the grandiloquent style of the era's poetry, and they manipulated the same figures from the communal rhetorical arsenal. Certainly, Abu Tammam demonstrated keen attention to the acoustic effects of his verse and was able to turn an aphorism as well as al-Mutanabbi. Neither he nor al-Buhturi could be faulted for lack of that Bedouin flavor and pre-Islamic cultural connection that the critics and aficionados found so appealing. Surely no poet was more associated than Abu Tammam with the use of philosophically oriented and logic-based conceits that often involved excursions into the paradoxical and the fantastic. And, like al-Mutanabbi, he loved his hyperbole. The most obvious response to this objection would have to be that in no poet of the period other than al-Mutanabbi do we find *all* these characteristics so expertly represented.

Yet the real key to al-Mutanabbi's uniqueness lies elsewhere, in his persistent presentation in his poems of an individual poetic voice. In an 'Abbasid poetic tradition dominated by convention and a firmly established set of social values and rules for patron – poet exchange, al-Mutanabbi's emphasis on individual experience breathed fresh life into an overly determined artistic environment. The degree to which an individual personality dealing with universal human emotions such as grief comes across in al-Mutanabbi's verse would have been revolutionary enough. But al-Mutanabbi goes further, for in his verse the interpretive framework for such emotion is precisely the heroic *Zeitgeist* that is the foundation of the dominant praise poetry. The vocal, flawed, struggling 'I' of al-Mutanabbi's verse judges itself by the norms ritually applied to the patron in official panegyric. The poet's ego – or the personal persona of his poems – often replaces the patron as the focal point of the panegyric, thus undermining the authority of the genre itself.

In al-Mutanabbi's poetry, the individual engages the abstract values the poetry articulates and attempts to live them. Failing that, he struggles to reconcile himself to the decisions he has made and justify his choices. Given the fact that praise of the patron is often little more than a poetic lie, the poet, thus often winds up being held to a higher standard than his paying client. Of course, the poet's claims about his own merits can be just as mendacious. The key difference between him and the patron, however, is that, because the poet lacks the free pass that wealth and power allow his patrons, al-Mutanabbi's claims invite verification in the events and accomplishments of his life. In this way, al-Mutanabbi actualizes the ethic espoused in his poetry in a way the power structure itself does not.

This attempt to mobilize the heroic code that dominated 'Abbasid panegyric poetry is the most unique – and subversive – aspect of al-Mutanabbi's *oeuvre*, for the communal and the personal, the private and the public are brought together in his poetry, as in no other 'Abbasid poet's work, to give life to the rhetorically dominant cultural ideal. It makes sense that our poet made ample use of irony, for it allowed him to bring out the tension and conflict that often result from the collision of communal values and individual realities and ambitions. There is thus a certain justice in the fact that al-Mutanabbi, the person, has become as important a cultural icon as al-Mutanabbi, the poet. And it is not surprising that both al-Mutanabbi and his verse have been engaged inter-textually by modern Arab poets who recognized themselves in the poet's personal and political conflicts, as they did the seeds of their modernist project in his persistent creation of personal voice. Al-Mutanabbi's idealism and ethnic chauvinism have made him the iconic focal point for modern plays, novels, and poetry dealing with nationalism and political resistance. His pessimism and personal angst resonate with ordinary people and artists alike. Ultimately, the range of passion and diversity of inspiration that al-Mutanabbi's *oeuvre* has occasioned over the past eleven centuries bear witness to the accuracy of Adunis' characterization of al-Mutanabbi's poetry as a "record of the sublime humanity of the individual."

SUGGESTIONS FOR FURTHER READING

IN ARABIC

Abu Sutayt, Shahata Muhammad. *Al-Ma'rakah al-naqdiyyah bayna Ibn Waki' wa 'l-Mutanabbi*. Cairo: Matba'at al-Amanah, 1991.

Adunis. *al-Kitab: Ams al-makan al-ana. Makhtutah tunsab ila al-Mutanabbi*. 3 vols. London: Dar al-Saqi, 1995–2002.

'Awwad, Kurkis and Mikha'il. *Ra'id al-dirasah 'an al-Mutanabbi*. Baghdad: 1977 (?).

al-Badi'i, Yusuf. *al-Subh al-munabbi*. 2nd ed. Cairo: Dar al-Ma'arif, 1977.

al-Barudi, Mahmud Sami. *Diwan al-Barudi*. Edited by 'Ali al-Jarim and Muhammad Shafiq Ma'ruf. Cairo: al-Hay'ah al-Misriyyah al-'Ammah li 'l-Kitab, 1992.

al-Bayyati, 'Abd al-Wahhab. *Diwan 'Abd al-Wahhab al-Bayyati*. Beirut: Dar al-'Awdah, 1971.

Darwish, Mahmud. *Hisar li-mada'ih al-bahr*. Amman: al-Dar al-'Arabiyyah li 'l-Nashr wa'l-Tawzi', 1986.

Dunqul, Amal. *al-A'mal al-shi'riyyah*. Cairo: Maktabat Madbuli, n.d.

al-Hatimi, Abu 'Ali Muhammad. *al-Risalah al-mudihah fi dhikr sariqat Abi al-Tayyib al-Mutanabbi wa-saqit shi'rihi*. Edited by Muhammad Yusuf Najm. Beirut: Dar Bayrut, 1965.

Husayn, Taha. *Ma'a al-Mutanabbi*. 12th ed. Cairo: Dar al-Ma'arif, 1980.

Ibn Hani' al-Andalusi, Muhammad. *Diwan Ibn Hani' al-Andalusi*. Beirut: Dar al-Gharb al-Islami, 1994.

Ibn Rashiq al-Qayrawani, Abu'l-Hasan. *al-'Umdah fi mahasin al-shi'r wa-adabih wa-naqdih*. Edited by Muhammad Muhyi al-Din 'Abd al-Hamid. 5th ed. Beirut: Dar al-Jil, 1981.

Ibn Waki', Abu Muhammad al-Hasan. *al-Munsif fi naqd al-shi'r wa-bayan sariqat al-Mutanabbi wa-mushkil shi'rih*. Edited by Muhammad Radwan al-Dayah. Damascus: Dar Qutaybah, 1982.

al-Jurjani, al-Qadi 'Ali ibn 'Abd al-'Aziz. *al-Wasatah bayna al-Mutanabbi wa-khusumih*. Edited by Muhammad Abu'l-Fadl Ibrahim and 'Ali Muhammad al-Bijawi. Cairo: Matba'at 'Isa al-Babi al-Halabi wa-Shurakah, n.d.

al-Ma'arri, Abu'l-'Ala'. *Diwan Saqt al-zand*. Cairo: Matba'at Hindiyyah, 1901.

al-Mutanabbi, Abu'l-Tayyib. *Diwan Abi'l-Tayyib al-Mutanabbi bi-sharh al-Abi'l-Baqa' al-'Ukbari*. Edited by Mustafa al-Saqqa, Ibrahim al-Abyari, and 'Abd al-Hafiz Shalabi. Offset reprint. Beirut: Dar al-Ma'rifah, 1978.

———. *Diwan Abi'l-Tayyib al-Mutanabbi*. Edited by 'Abd al-Rahman al-Barquqi. Beirut: Dar al-Kitab al-'Arabi, 1980.

———. *Diwan Abi'l-Tayyib al-Mutanabbi bi-sharh al-Wahidi*. Edited by F. Dieterici. Berlin: 1861.

———. *Sharh diwan Abi'l-Tayyib*. Edited by Nasif al-Yaziji. Beirut: Dar Sadir, n.d.

———. *Sharh diwan Abi'l-Tayyib al-Mutanabbi li-Abi'l-'Ala' al-Ma'arri*. Edited by 'Abd al-Majid Diyab. 2nd ed. Cairo: Dar al-Ma'arif, 1992.

Shakir, Mahmud Muhammad. *Al-Mutanabbi*. 2 vols. Cairo: Matba'at al-Madani, 1976.

Shawqi, Ahmad. *Diwan Shawai*. Cairo: Dar Nahdat-Misr-li'l-Tab'wa'l-Nashr, n. d.

al-Tha'alibi, Abu Mansur 'Abd al-Malik. *Yatimat al-dahr fi mahasin ahl al-'asr*. Edited by Muhammad Muhyi al-Din 'Abd al-Hamid. 2nd ed. Cairo: Matba'at al-Sa'adah, 1956.

IN ENGLISH

Arberry, A. J. *Poems of al-Mutanabbi: A Selection with Introduction, Translations and Notes*. Cambridge: Cambridge University Press, 1967.

Ashtiany, Julia. "Mutanabbi's Elegy on Sayf al-Dawla's Son." In *Festschrift Ewald Wagner zum 65. Geburtstag*, edited by Wolfhart Heinrichs and Gregor Schoeler, 362–372. Beirut: Franz Steiner, 1994.

Bonebakker, S. A. *Hatimi and his Encounter with Mutanabbi: A Biographical Sketch*. Amsterdam: North-Holland, 1984.

Gelder, Geert Jan van. "Al-Mutanabbi, the Long and the Short of It: al-Mutanabbi's Encumbering Trifles." *Arabic and Middle Eastern Literatures*, vol. 2, no. 1 (1999): 5–19.

Grunebaum, Gustave E. von. 'The Concept of Plagiarism in Arabic Theory." *Journal of Near Eastern Studies*, vol. 3, no. 1 (1944): 234–253.

Hamori, Andras. *The Composition of Mutanabbi's Panegyrics to Sayf al-Dawla*. Leiden: E.J. Brill, 1992.

———. *On the Art of Arabic Literature*. Princeton: Princeton University Press, 1974.

———. "Al-Mutanabbi." In *Cambridge History of Arabic Literature: 'Abbasid Belles-Lettres*, edited by Julia Ashtiany, T. M. Johnstone, J. D. Latham, R. B. Serjeant, and G. Rex Smith, 300–314. Cambridge: Cambridge University Press, 1990.

———. "Reading al-Mutanabbi's Ode on the Siege of al-Hadat." In *Studia Arabica et Islamica: Festschrift for Ishan 'Abbas*, edited by Wadad al-Qadi, 195–206. Beirut: American University of Beirut, 1981.

Heinrichs, Wolfhart. "The Meaning of Mutanabbi." In *Poetry and Prophecy: The Beginnings of a Literary Tradition*, edited by James L. Kugel, 120–139. Ithaca, New York: Cornell University Press, 1990.

Larkin, Margaret. "Two Examples of Ritha': A Comparison of al-Mutanabbi and Shawqi." *Journal of Arabic Literature*, vol. 16 (1986): 18–39.

Latham, J. Derek. "Towards a Better Understanding of al-Mutanabbi's Poem on the Battle of al-Hadath." *Journal of Arabic Literature*, vol. 10 (1979): 1–22.

Linthicum, Nancy. "Mahmoud Darwish Indicts Modern Arab Poets." *Al Jadid: A Review of Arab Culture and Arts*, vol. 11, nos. 50/51 (2005): 14–17.

Meisami, Julie Scott. "Al-Mutanabbi and the Critics." *Arabic and Middle Eastern Literatures*, vol. 2, no. 1 (1999): 21–41.

Montgomery, James E. "Al-Mutanabbi and the Psychology of Grief." *Journal of the American Oriental Society*, vol. 115, no. 2 (1995): 285–292.

Nicholson, Reynold A. *A Literary History of the Arabs*. Cambridge: Cambridge University Press, 1914.

Sperl, Stefan. *Mannerism in Arabic Poetry*. Cambridge: Cambridge University Press, 1989.

Sperl, Stefan and Christopher Shackle, eds. *Qasida Poetry in Islamic Asia and Africa*, vol. 1, *Classical Traditions and Modern Meanings*. Leiden: E.J. Brill, 1996.

Stetkevych, Suzanne P. "The Poetics of Political Allegiance: Praise and Blame in Three Odes by al-Mutanabbi." In *The Poetics of Islamic Legitimacy*, 180–240. Bloomington: Indiana University Press, 2002.

IN OTHER LANGUAGES

Al Mutanabbi: Recueil publié à l'occasion de son millénaire. Beirut: l'Institut français de Damas, 1936.

Blachère, Régis. *Un poète arabe du IVe siècle de l'Hégire (Xe de J.-C.): Abou t-Tayyib al-Motanabbi: Essai d'histoire littéraire.* Paris: Librairie d'Amérique et d'Orient, 1935.

Mahfuz, Husayn 'Ali. *Mutanabbi va Sa'di va Ma'khaz-i mazamin-i Sa'di dar adabiyat-i 'arabi.* Tehran: Intisharat-i Rawzanah, 1957.

INDEX

A

'Abassid era
   al-Mutanabbi, appearance of 11–12
   Arabic letters, heyday of 8–9
   caliphate, breakup of 11–12
   panegyric poetry, in honor of caliphs 9–10
   Ummayad rulers, capitalization on frustration with 8–9
Abu'l-Fadl 16–17
Abu'l-Hayja' 46–50
adolescent defiance 23
al-Raffa', al-Sariy 105
alcohol, al-Mutanabbi's dislike of 22, 26–7
amatory preludes 17–18, 35, 47–8, 87
antithesis, use of 11, 19, 54
aphorisms 104, 105, 119, 127, 128
Arberry, A.J. xiii
al-'Arudi 103
'l-'Asha'ir, Abu'l 35, 60, 103
Ashtiany (now Bray) 50
assonance 55
'l-'Atahiyah, Abu 9, 56
'Awwad, Kurkis and Mikha'il xiii

B

Baghdad
   heroic patron, al-Mutanabbi's longing for 13–14
   imperial court, as vibrant cultural centre 9
   literary efflorescence in xi
   loss of as symbol of Arab cultural unity 12–13
   al-Mutanabbi's time in 17–20
   poets, effect on 13
   return to 78–9
al-Barudi, Mahmud Sami 118–21
al-Basri, Ali 85, 95, 97
battles, panegyric descriptions of 52–3
al-Bayyati, 'Abd al-Wahhab 125
Blachère, Régis xiii, 35, 49, 68
boasting 29, 52, 58, 70–2, 116–17
Bonebakker, S.A. 79, 104
Bray, Julia (Ashtiany) xiii
al-Buhturi 15, 55, 90, 99, 104, 105, 110, 114, 118, 128
Buyid dynasty 13–14, 78, 84, 87, 90, 92, 100, 104
Byzantine domesticus and army, lampooning of 55

C

caliphs, mythologizing of 9–10
ceremonial occasions, odes on 53
classical Arabic tradition xi, 120–1
   see also neoclassical poetry
conceits
   criticism of 105–6
   novelty of 105
   patron's title, playing on 40–1
   Sufi poetry 103–4
conservatism, in poetic taste
   manneristic poetry 11
   'new style *(badi')* poetry 11
   rationalism, Hellenist-inspired 11
   tripartite ode 10–11
court poetry 3
critical treatises, following death of al-Mutanabbi 110–11

D

Dabis, Abu 22
Darwish, Mahmud 122, 124–5
al-Dawlah, Adud xiv, 13, 87, 93
al-Dawlah, Mu'izz 78, 105
al-Dawlah, Sayf xiv, 13, 26, 31–2, 33–4, 63, 64, 70
  apology poem to 57–8
  court of 34
  disappointment and abandonment 60
  disavowal of 63–5
  epic occasions, poems for 54–6
  first ode to 35–41
  invitation back to court, poem in response to 84
  mother, elegy to 43–4
  al-Mutanabbi, agitation against 57–60
  al-Mutanabbi's respect for 34
  occasional poems for 41–3
  onomatopoeia, use of 55
  patron's title, conceit of playing on 40–1
  poem of thanks to 81
  poem on death of 72–3
  poet, demands on 52–4
  poet-patron relationship 50–2
  polythematic ode 35
  propaganda poetry 56
  public *versus* private domains of 48–9
  rhetorical powers, reminder of 59–60
  sister, elegy to 82–3, 105
  son, elegy to 46–50
debates, participation in 53–4
detractors, al-Mutanabbi's mocking of 60–1
diction
  classic Arab odes 89
  lexical choice 99–101
  manipulation of the music of 55–6
Diwan (Collected Poetry) al-Mutanabbi xiii
double-entendre 11
Dunqul, Amal 122–4

E

economy of expression 19
elegies
  influence on Ahmad Shawqi 121–2
  as panegyric in the past tense 51
  poet's greatness as vehicle for recovery from grief 27–9
  to Sayf al-Dawlah's mother 46–50
  to Sayf al-Dawlah's sister 82–3, 105
  to Sayf al-Dawlah's son 46–50
emotional power xii
eulogy of patron, as eulogy of poet 51–2
excellence, recognition of 109–10

F

al-Farabi 34
fate 4, 49, 83, 105
Firas, Abu 57–60

G

'Gap of Bavvan'
  beauty of the glade, paean to 90–2
  diction, and classic Arab odes 89
  ode in farewell 95
  panegyric section 92–3
  Persian and Arab abodes, contrast between 92
  poetic persona, and tension between Arab and Persian culture 89–90
Gelder, G.J. van xiii
al-Ghuri, Lu'lu' 24
gnomic verses, structural and rhetorical features of 54
gnostic Shi'ites 17, 24
grandmother, death of
  boasting 29
  elegy on 27–9, 121–2
  fate, and existential responsibility 29, 30
  individual distinction, focus on 29–30
  narrative features, and use of verb tenses 28–9
Guide to the Study of al-Mutanabbi ('Awwad) xiii

H

ha-Levi, Judah 113–14
al-Hamdani, Abu Firas 34, 57–60, 94
Hamdanids, of Aleppo 33–4
Hamori, Andras xiii, 17, 44–5
al-Hasan of Ramala 63, 76
al-Hatimi 104–5
Hebrew verse, influence of Arabic poetry on 113–14
Heinrichs, Wolfhart 24
Hellenistic philosophy 11, 17
heroic self-portraits 22, 70–2, 77–8
hospitality, images of Arab 91–2
hunt poems
  panegyric 94–5
  'quick' meter 94
Husayn, Taha xiii
hyperbole 74–5, 94–5, 106–7, 128

I

Ibn 'Abbad, al-Sahib 100–1, 103
Ibn Abi al-Jahl, Fatik 95
Ibn Ahmad , 'Ali ibn Ahmad 'Amir al-Antaki 114
Ibn al-Hasan al-Hatami, 'Ali Muhammad 64, 79, 104–5
Ibn al-'Amid, Abu'l Fadl Muhammad 84–7
Ibn Bashshar, Burd 11, 108
Ibn Hani' 114–16
Ibn Hinzaba 109
Ibn Ishak al-Tanukhi al-Husayn, Ishaq 108
Ibn Jinni 85, 96, 97–8, 109, 111
Ibn Kayghulugh, Ishaq 31, 32
Ibn Khalawayh 34, 62, 116
Ibn al-Khurasani, Ahmad 100
Ibn Malik 63
Ibn al-Muhallabi, Muhammad 78, 105
Ibn al-Mu'tazz 11, 109
Ibn al-Qayrawani, Rashiq 106
Ibn Qutaybah 6
Ibn Rashiq 1
Ibn al-Rumi 128
Ibn Rushdayn, Salih 97

Ibn Tugh al-Ikhshidid, Muhammad 66
Ibn 'Ubayd Allah, Abu Muhammad al-Hasan 17, 31
Ibn Waki', Abu Muhammad al-Hasan 98–9, 108, 111
Ibn al-Walid, Muslim 11
Ibn Yazid al-'Utubi, Dabba 95
Ikhshidid connection 30–1
imagination
  conceits 105–6
  hyperbole 106–7
Imru'l-Qays 47
individual verses, quotability of 31–2
individual voice
  panegyric poetry 32
  presence of in poetry 21
  uniqueness of al-Mutanabbi 128–9
intertextuality, in Arab literary tradition xiii, xiv, 3, 120–1, 129
invective 3–4
irony 129
al-Isfahani, Abu'l-Faraj 78–9
Islam, effect on poetry 5–6

J

al-Jurjani, 'Abd al-Qahir 106, 109
al-Jurjani, al-Qadi 102, 104, 105

K

Kafur, Abu'l Misk 63–78
Kafur, Abu'l-Misk as patron
  Arab racial superiority, of al-Mutanabbi 67
  blasphemy 67
  equivocal praise 64, 65–9
  Fustat, escape from 76–8
  hyperbole, ludicrous nature of 74–5
  insults, and heroic self-image 70–2, 77–8
  invective, boldly uncensored 77
  Kafur's lowly origins 67–8
  mockery 68, 74, 75
  panegyric, first 63–6, 101
  poet-patron relationship 69

political appointment, promise of 69–75
racist invective against 75–6
al-Kharshani, Isma'il 26–7
al-Khasibi, 'Abd Allah 27

L

laments 3–4
Latham, J. Derek 56
lexical choice 99–101
life and death
   metaphors, use of 44–5
   undermining of distinction between 46–7
linguistic correctness 98–9
lost abode of beloved 2, 10, 18, 36–7
love poetry 2, 8
   'Abassid 36–7
   of al-Mutanabbi 82–3
   Arabic 40
   language of 44–7

M

al-Ma'arri, Abu'l 'Ala' 111, 116–17
manneristic poetry 11, 39–40
memorization, facilitation of 31–2, 127
metaphysical poets (English) 11
meter 2, 4, 46–7
modern Arab poets, influence of al-Mutanabbi on 110, 122, 126
modernist Arabic poetry xi
Montgomery, James xiii
mount, poet's
   description of 18
   symbolism of 2, 10
Mu'adh, Abu 'Abd Allah 23, 24
al-Muhallabi 78–9
Muhammad 6, 7
al-Muhassad 95
al-Mu'izz, li-Din Allah 114, 115
al-Murtada 116
al-Mutanabbi, Abu'l-Tayyib xi
   birth of 15
   death of 95–6

emergence of 11–12
imprisonment of 24–5
as inspiration xi–xiii
oeuvre, transmission and study of 97–8, 110–11
poverty of upbringing 15–16
studies of xiii
mythic beloved and poet's sponsor, blurring of distinction between 37–9
mythologizing, of caliphs 9–10

N

al-Nami, Abu'l-'Abbas 98, 105
al-Nasir, 'Abd 123–34
neoclassical poetry
   aphorisms, use of 119
   Arabic literary 'renaissance' 118
   boasting 118
   classical Arabic poetic tradition, evocation of 120–1
   conceits 119–20
   direct citations 118
   elegy to grandmother, influence of 121–2
   gnomic lines 119
   meter and rhyme letter 118
   al-Mutanabbi poem as model 118–21
   phrasing and diction 118
   romantic school 117–18
'new style (badi') poetry 11
Nuwas, Abu 9, 10, 94, 118

O

odes
   Ibn 'Ubayd Allah, polythematic ode to 17–20
   panegyric poetry 9–10, 13
   polythematic 2–3, 35, 46
   tribe, propaganda and publicity for (polythematic ode) 3, 8
   tripartite ode 10–11
onomatopoeia, use of 55
originality, quest for 42–3

'outlaw' (*sa'alik*) poets 4–5, 18, 70

P

panegyric poetry
   'Abassid era 9–10
   elegy, as panegyric in the past tense 51
   Gap of Bavvan poem 92–3
   hyperbole 94–5
   individual voice of poet 32
   to Kafur 63–6, 101
   odes 9–10, 13
   panegyrist, difficult position of 42
paronomasia 55
patron, material and spiritual authority of 20
Persians, as major practitioners of poetry 9, 10
personality, complex of al-Mutanabbi 20–2
pessimism 117
philosophizing, in poetry 128
   al-Hatimi, debate with 104–5
   aphorisms, praise for 104, 105
   apostasy, accusations of 103
   Sufis, 'difficult language and ambiguous conceits of' 103–4
plagiarism, *versus* borrowing 127
   originality, and tradition 107
   poetic borrowing, systems for 107–8
   poetic competition 109
   poetry, communal nature of 107
poems
   'Because of you, we, above the ground . . .' 46–50
   'Feast day, in what state do you return . . .' 77
   'Go easy, lofty prince . . .' 41–3
   'I understand your letter . . .' 84
   'I used to wish that white hair . . .' 70, 102
   'I wanted from the days that which they do not like . . .' 118–21
   'It is sickness enough . . .' 63–6, 101
   'May he who falls short . . .' 95
   'Oh sister of the best of brothers . . .' 83, 105
   'Resolutions occur according to the measure of the people of resolve . . .' 54–6
   'Verily every woman sashaying . . .' 77–8
   'What's wrong with us, oh messenger . . .' 81
   'Where have you resolved to go . . .' 41–3
   'With what can I distract myself . . .' 72–3
   'Your love is apparent . . .' 85–7
poet
   primitive individuality 5
   as publicist and political propagandist 51
   as tribal representative 3
   wealth and status of 51–2
   as wise guide 51–2
poetic canon, mastery of 42
pre-Islamic poetry 1
   corpus, incompleteness of 4
   as model of excellence 6
prophet, al-Mutanabbi as would-be 23–4, 117
punning 11

Q

Qur'an
   Muhammad as seal of prophets 23
   word of God and Arabic language, connection between 5–6

R

al-Raffa', al-Sariy
Rahbani, Mansour xiii
al-Rashid, Harun 9
rationalism, Hellenist-inspired 11
representation, preoccupation with 39–40
romantic school 117–18
rugged manliness theme 5

S

Sa'di, influence on 113
Sa'id, 'Ali Ahmad (Adunis), and role of poet/poetry in society 126, 129
satire/invective poems 22
Shackle, Christopher 67
Shakir, Mahmud xiii, 43
Sharran, Ta'abbata 5
Shawqi, Ahmad 121–2
Sperl, Stefan 67
spur of the moment pieces 53
Stetkevych, Suzanne xiii, 63
structure, poetic 101–2
style, originality of 110
Sufi poetry 103–4

T

Tammam, Abu 11, 15, 20, 54, 55, 56, 91, 99, 104, 105, 110, 114, 118, 128
al-Tawhidi 111

al-Tha'alibi 99–100, 106, 110
transitions 102
translations xii–xiv
tribe, propaganda and publicity for 1, 2–3, 6, 8

U

al-'Ukbari 98
Umayyads, centralization under 7–8

W

al-Wahidi xiii, 103, 110
Wakin, Jeanette xii
wine-song 8
wisdom, poet as voice of 49–50

Y

Yemenite origins 15

Z

al-Zayyat, Ahmad 117